3-17-2019: FO...

TO... P9-CFT-082

OF INCREASED

CONSCIOUSNESS!

— বাবা au.

The

Mindfulness

Survival Kit

The
Mindfulness
Survival Kit

PARALLAX
PRESS

Berkeley, California

THICH NHAT HANH

Parallax Press
P.O. Box 7355
Berkeley, California 94707
www.parallax.org

Parallax Press is the publishing division of
Unified Buddhist Church, Inc.

Edited by Rachel Neumann
Cover design by Anne Nguyen
Interior design by Elaine Chow
Author photo © Richard Friday

Printed on 100% post-consumer waste recycled paper

Nhât Hanh, Thích.
 The mindfulness survival kit : five essential practices /
Thích Nhât Hanh.
    pages cm
 ISBN 978-1-937006-34-1
 1. Meditation--Buddhism. I. Title.
 BQ9800.T5392N454613 2013
 294.3'4435--dc23
                                    2013033104

4 5 6 / 18 17 16

CONTENTS

Part 1

A Mindfulness
Survival Kit

Mindfulness can help us survive and thrive, both as individuals and as human beings on this Earth together.

CHAPTER 1

Why We Need a Mindfulness Survival Kit

Mindfulness is the awareness of what is going on in us and around us in the present moment. It requires stopping, looking deeply, and recognizing both the uniqueness of the moment and its connection to everything that has gone on before and will go on in the future. Mindfulness can help us survive and thrive, both as individuals and as human beings on this Earth together. Mindfulness is a continual practice—a path that helps us to transform our suffering and that brings happiness to ourselves and to others.

This book contains a modern, updated, and secular version of the Buddha's teaching of the Five Precepts, the Buddha's guidelines for an ethical life. In 1985, we revised the Five Mindfulness

Trainings to reflect the way people were living at that time. But now, more than twenty-five years later, it is time to look at them again. We have to revise them in such a way that whenever we recite them we can see the practice of concentration and insight in them. In another twenty or thirty years' time, perhaps we shall need to revise them again as the world continues to change and transform. The essence stays the same, but the form may be different.

My hope is that these Mindfulness Trainings can represent a Buddhist contribution to a global ethic, a way for the human species to sustain itself in these dangerous and difficult times. After almost seventy years of practice, I have found these Mindfulness Trainings can help relieve suffering and produce happiness by helping us generate the energies of mindfulness, concentration, and insight. The practice of these three energies can open the door to liberate people from the prison of their suffering.

The Chinese and Vietnamese word for religion is *jiao*, which means a tradition of teachings. In Eastern cultures, religion does not imply a belief in God. *Tao* is the Chinese word for path or Way. The Mindfulness Teachings are a wide path out of suffering, not necessarily connected with a particular religion. Buddhism was developed as a teaching path, rather than a religion. The first teaching the Buddha gave was to his five friends who used to practice self-mortification with him. That teaching, called the Setting in Motion of the Dharma Wheel, was to become the foundation of a new ethics and morality that consists of the Four Noble Truths and the Noble Eightfold Path. Ethics are principles of action that will reduce suffering and nourish happiness.

THE FOUR NOBLE TRUTHS

In his first teaching, the Buddha spoke of the Four Noble Truths. These are ill-being, the path leading to ill-being, well-being, and the path leading to well-being. The Fourth Noble Truth, the path leading to well-being, is called the Noble Eightfold Path. This is the path of the Eight Right Practices: Right View, Right Thinking, Right Speech, Right Action (of the body), Right Livelihood, Right

Diligence, Right Mindfulness, Right Concentration. If we look deeply enough, these four truths contain everything we need to know about the nature of being human and the nature of the world around us. If we see the true nature of the Four Noble Truths, we shall see the true nature of the cosmos.

One thing you can always be sure of is that there is suffering in us and in the world. The Buddha built his teaching and practice based on that truth. We know that if suffering is there, something else must also be there and that is happiness. Just understanding and accepting this truth can bring us some relief. Our ill-being, our suffering, is not exactly our fault. It's the result of many causes and conditions, both collective and individual—such as wrong perceptions, confusion, and strong emotions, which lead to unskillful actions of body, speech, and mind. That doesn't mean that happiness can't exist. We don't have to destroy suffering in order to have happiness.

When we accept the First Noble Truth (there is ill-being), we can practice two things. First, we can acknowledge the real suffering in us and around us. Second, we can learn to handle the suffering that we have acknowledged.

Acknowledging suffering doesn't mean that we have to see *everything* as suffering or that it's enough to intellectually see that there is suffering. Identifying suffering as it is means that we don't run away from it and we take steps to be able to transform it. In order to transform suffering, we have to look deeply into it and find its roots. If there's tension in the body, we can identify it and discover its roots in order to ease it. If we know that the stress comes from the fact that we work too hard, for example, and are too distracted to dwell in the present moment, we can find a way to bring ease and rest into our day. If instead we ignore our stress, and just think that if we only work more we can take care of everything, then every day we add stress to stress and store it up in our body. If we continue like this, we make ourselves sick. If we start by being gentle with ourselves, giving ourselves time to return to ourselves in the present moment, we can begin to heal.

When we look into the First Noble Truth, the Second Noble Truth appears. The Second Noble

Truth is the causes of our ill-being. When we look into ill-being deeply, we can see how it has developed. The Second Noble Truth illuminates the path that has led us to suffering.

One of the deepest causes of our suffering is our insistence on seeing reality in a dualistic way and our attachment to our beliefs. Ethics is the capacity to distinguish between right and wrong. Often, we're caught in our beliefs about what's right and wrong. We get stuck in wrong views and lose our way. We may think, for example, "That person wants to kill us. If we don't kill him first, he will certainly kill us. So we have to find a way to kill him first." But this kind of thinking may be based entirely on suspicion, fear, and wrong perceptions.

Wrong views lead to wrong thinking, and wrong thinking leads to wrong speech and wrong bodily action, whereby we bring violence to ourselves and to others. With wrong view, we may find ourselves living with wrong livelihood, earning our living by destroying the natural environment; by depriving others of the chance to live; or by lying and persuading others to buy our merchandise although we know that it's harmful for their health. Wrong view also leads to wrong diligence, whereby we may work very hard day and night thinking that will bring us success and happiness, and we leave no time for our families and ourselves. In this way, we store up stress in our bodies and anxiety in our minds. Wrong view leads to wrong mindfulness. For example we may spend our days preoccupied with how to make more money or have more power and fame. We are never present in the here and the now because we're always running after the object of our desire. Wrong view can also lead to wrong concentration, which means we focus on ideas and notions that cause us ill-being and we think of others as being completely unconnected to us.

When we think of the Second Noble Truth, the causes of suffering, many of us think of the external causes and structures of poverty, disease, unemployment, social injustice, slavery, and discrimination. These are real causes that beget enormous suffering. If we look deeply, we shall see that this kind of suffering is not separate from the personal suffering of individuals. Even if there were no poverty, disease, unemployment, and social injustice, it wouldn't mean there would be no more stress, worry, fear, and violence. There would still be suffering. But if we knew how to handle our stress, worry, fear, and anger, then violence would diminish. We have to look deeply to know the real roots of our suffering. Some people come from poverty and violence and find financial success. But if there is still worry, stress, fear, and anger they will continue to suffer even though they have been successful in the worldly sense.

Our societies are organized in such a way that every day the stress becomes greater. The majority of our suffering comes about because of stress. When there is no stress we can resolve things in a peaceful way, without irritation. Stress is an element that can be found wherever there is poverty, fear, anxiety, violence, broken families, divorce, suicide, war, conflict, and environmental pollution. Stress is also linked to the personal suffering in people's hearts, including our relationships with our ancestors, our descendants, and our loved ones, which is a suffering that is so great that it's not possible to recount it all. Suffering has many faces. If we discover the roots of one suffering, we are at the same time discovering the roots of other suffering, and we'll start to see that each suffering has many causes and not just one root. When we recognize the origins of our suffering, we are able to transform that suffering.

The Third Noble Truth is that there is an end of ill-being. This means that suffering can be transformed into happiness. The Third Truth is the confirmation that well-being is possible, happiness is possible, peace is possible. The Third Noble Truth implies that there's a path that leads to well-being. This in itself is a very significant statement. Transformation and happiness are possible. We don't have to stay stuck.

The Fourth Noble Truth is the path leading to well-being, When we look into the nature of ill-being, we may begin to see not only the path that led to our suffering, but the path leading away from our suffering, the path that leads to well-being. You need only to look into one truth in order to see all the other three truths. In the Buddhist tradition, the path that leads to well-being is called the Noble Eightfold Path. It is noble because it leads us to peace, compassion, love, and happiness. The practice of the Noble Eightfold Path can transform ill-being into well-being.

The Noble Eightfold Path is made up of eight practices that lead to the transformation of suffering. The path begins with Right View. In the Buddhist tradition, there is the practice of demolishing attachment to views. So "Right View" means we don't allow ourselves to be caught in any kind of idealism, theories, or systems of thought, even Buddhist ones. The Buddha describes each of the eight practices of the Noble Path as "Right" to indicate that they are practices that go in the direction of well-being and happiness.

Sometimes Right View is also referred to as insight or wisdom (*prajña* in Sanskrit). Right View isn't bestowed on us from some deity or absolute power; it comes from the practice of looking deeply inside ourselves. We use mindfulness and concentration to examine the Four Noble Truths and arrive at Right View. As long as we think and believe that our actions are right according to God, or right according to even the best of ideologies, we will remain caught in the wheel of suffering.

Right View is the absence of all attachment to views. Right View is the insight of interbeing. Interbeing describes the awareness that all human beings and all phenomena are intricately connected to each other and interdependent. None of us can be by ourselves alone; we have to inter-be with all living beings. We inter-are with all animals, plants, and minerals. If you do harm to animals, plants, and minerals, you do harm to yourself. With this insight, when you look deeply into another human being, you see the animals, plants, and minerals that contribute to making up his or her being, and therefore you think and act differently than you would otherwise.

When there is Right View, Right Thinking follows. Right Speech and Right Bodily Action also depend on Right View. Body, speech, and mind are all sources of action. Every day our bodies, our speech, and our minds produce a tremendous number of actions. These actions can contribute to healing or to suffering. When we give rise to a thought of forgiveness or compassion, it's Right

Thinking. If we give rise to a thought of anger, hatred, or despondency, it's wrong thinking. Every day we talk, we write, and we send emails or texts. What we write and say can be Right Speech, bringing ourselves and the other person happiness or it can be wrong speech and bring suffering and misunderstanding.

We use our bodies to act. When our bodily action protects and supports life, it is Right Action. With Right View, we can choose a vocation that nourishes ourselves, our loved ones, and the planet, rather than one that brings about the destruction of the environment and harm to other species. That is Right Livelihood. When we're diligent in serving our own and others' happiness, it's Right Diligence. These eight right practices can be seen as the basis of Buddhist ethics that can be applied in society. We cannot live in isolation. We always need to be in contact with other people and other species. With the practice of the Noble Eightfold Path we avoid the actions of body, speech, and mind that will harm others.

When we practice Right Mindfulness, we use our breathing to return to ourselves and unite body and mind. When we walk, we walk with awareness and not because something is pulling us along. When we say something, it's because it's what we truly want to say and not because our old habit energies are urging us to say it. Mindfulness strengthens our sovereignty over ourselves. As mindfulness and concentration grow, our freedom also grows. The more we practice, the less our freedom is limited. We become free of drifting and sinking with the currents of our mind.

The Third Noble Truth, the cessation of suffering, reminds us that we have the ability to change the direction of our lives. This means that we have free will. Right Mindfulness leads to Right Concentration, which supports and strengthens insight and Right View. So the path is a circular path, with each limb of the path leading to and supporting the other limbs. There is suffering, but there is also happiness. We can practice to reduce suffering and to increase happiness.

The Five Mindfulness Trainings are a way to practice the Four Noble Truths and the Noble Eightfold Path in daily life. The trainings aren't commandments given by a god or authority figure; they're ethical guidelines that reflect our own experience and insight. The trainings offer concrete ways of practice that deepen our understanding and help us see people, situations, and our environment more clearly. You don't need to be a Buddhist or call yourself a Buddhist to live according to the Five Mindfulness Trainings. I know many people from various religious traditions who have included the Five Mindfulness Trainings as part of their daily practice and code of personal conduct.

It is very helpful to have the support of a community that is practicing the trainings together. After enlightenment the first thing the Buddha did was to go out and search for elements of a *Sangha*, a spiritual community. Without a community, he couldn't realize his intention to be a teacher. We each need a community like this to help us practice. We benefit from the collective energy of mindfulness, which is stronger than our own individual energy. Together, we help the seeds of mindfulness, concentration, and insight to grow.

The Five Mindfulness Trainings are called trainings because they are something to practice each day, not something we're expected to do perfectly all the time. They are there to remind us of our aspiration and our commitment. Practicing them, we continue to learn and to deepen our practice and our understanding. Reading them periodically, once a month at least, will help us stay focused on the path toward well-being and ethical living. As with any training, it's helpful to have concrete practices to train with. Each training is followed by some commentary and a companion practice. Since each training contains all the others, any one of these practices will strengthen the way you practice all of them.

In the Buddhist tradition in which I practice, people don't just read the Five Mindfulness Trainings, they receive them from a teacher. People sometimes ask why we need to transmit the trainings in this way. It is enough to study and put them into practice for ourselves, but it's easier when we've made a public commitment and received support from a whole community to practice the trainings. Every day, we encounter so many messages and stimuli that are in contrast to the trainings. When we have the energy of a whole community that has witnessed us make a commitment to the trainings, it's easier to practice. We can draw on the strength of the collective consciousness.

Some people choose to focus on just one mindfulness training, such as Right Speech. It is perfectly good to pick just one training to focus on, because the one contains the all. Practicing Right Speech will lead us to practice Right Thinking, because sooner or later we shall say what we have been thinking. Practicing Right Thinking, we are also practicing the first mindfulness training on protecting life and respecting life. When we practice Right Speech deeply and we listen deeply and compassionately to someone, we feel we become one with them. We feel his or her suffering and we understand it. We see how his happiness and my happiness are not two separate things, and this is the second mindfulness training on True Happiness. Read the trainings with an awareness of your capacity and of what is possible. With one small commitment to mindfulness, you begin to water the seeds of transformation and joy.

Reverence for Life

GENEROSITY
True Happiness

KINDNESS, LOVING
True Love

Deep Listening and Loving Speech

INTERBEING
Nourishment and Healing

CHAPTER 2

The Five Mindfulness Trainings

THE FIRST MINDFULNESS TRAINING: REVERENCE FOR LIFE

Aware of the suffering caused by the destruction of life, I am committed to cultivating the insight of interbeing and compassion and learning ways to protect the lives of people, animals, plants, and minerals. I am determined not to kill, not to let others kill, and not to support any act of killing in the world, in my thinking, or in my way of life. Seeing that harmful actions arise from anger, fear, greed, and intolerance, which in turn come from dualistic and discriminative thinking, I will cultivate openness, nondiscrimination, and nonattachment to views in order to transform violence, fanaticism, and dogmatism in myself and in the world.

Aware of the suffering caused by exploitation, social injustice, stealing, and oppression, I am committed to practicing generosity in my thinking, speaking, and acting. I am determined not to steal and not to possess anything that should belong to others; and I will share my time, energy, and material resources with those who are in need. I will practice looking deeply to see that the happiness and suffering of others are not separate from my own happiness and suffering; that true happiness is not possible without understanding and compassion; and that running after wealth, fame, power, and sensual pleasures can bring much suffering and despair. I am aware that happiness depends on my mental attitude and not on external conditions, and that I can live happily in the present moment simply by remembering that I already have more than enough conditions to be happy. I am committed to practicing Right Livelihood so that I can help reduce the suffering of living beings on Earth and reverse the process of global warming.

Aware of the suffering caused by sexual misconduct, I am committed to cultivating responsibility and learning ways to protect the safety and integrity of individuals, couples, families, and society. Knowing that sexual desire is not love, and that sexual activity motivated by craving always harms myself as well as others, I am determined not to engage in sexual relations without true love and a deep, long-term commitment made known to my family and friends. I will do everything in my power to protect children from sexual abuse and to prevent couples and families from being broken by sexual misconduct. Seeing that body and mind are one, I am committed to learning appropriate ways to take care of my sexual energy and to cultivating loving kindness, compassion, joy, and inclusiveness—which are the four basic elements of true love—for my greater happiness and the greater happiness of others. Practicing true love, we know that we will continue beautifully into the future.

THE FOURTH MINDFULNESS TRAINING:
DEEP LISTENING AND LOVING SPEECH

Aware of the suffering caused by unmindful speech and the inability to listen to others, I am committed to cultivating loving speech and compassionate listening in order to relieve suffering and to promote reconciliation and peace in myself and among other people, ethnic and religious groups, and nations. Knowing that words can create happiness or suffering, I am committed to speaking truthfully using words that inspire confidence, joy, and hope. When anger is manifesting in me, I am determined not to speak. I will practice mindful breathing and walking in order to recognize and to look deeply into my anger. I know that the roots of anger can be found in my wrong perceptions and lack of understanding of the suffering in myself and in the other person. I will speak and listen in a way that can help myself and the other person to transform suffering and see the way out of difficult situations. I am determined not to spread news that I do not know to be certain and not to utter words that can cause division or discord.

I will practice Right Diligence to nourish my capacity for understanding, love, joy, and inclusiveness, and gradually transform anger, violence, and fear that lie deep in my consciousness.

Aware of the suffering caused by unmindful consumption, I am committed to cultivating good health, both physical and mental, for myself, my family, and my society by practicing mindful eating, drinking, and consuming. I will practice looking deeply into how I consume the Four Kinds of Nutriments, namely edible foods, sense impressions, volition, and consciousness. I am determined not to gamble, or to use alcohol, drugs, or any other products which contain toxins, such as certain websites, electronic games, TV programs, films, magazines, books, and conversations. I will practice coming back to the present moment to be in touch with the refreshing, healing, and nourishing elements in me and around me, not letting regrets and sorrow drag me back into the past nor letting anxieties, fear, or craving pull me out of the present moment. I am determined not to try to cover up loneliness, anxiety, or other suffering by losing myself in consumption. I will contemplate interbeing and consume in a way that preserves peace, joy, and well-being in my body and consciousness and in the collective body and consciousness of my family, my society, and the Earth.

The First Mindfulness Training

reminds us to protect life and

nourish compassion.

CHAPTER 3

The First Mindfulness Training: Reverence for Life

Aware of the suffering caused by the destruction of life, I am com-
mitted to cultivating the insight of interbeing and compassion and
learning ways to protect the lives of people, animals, plants, and
minerals. I am determined not to kill, not to let others kill, and
not to support any act of killing in the world, in my thinking, or
in my way of life. Seeing that harmful actions arise from anger,
fear, greed, and intolerance, which in turn come from dualistic
and discriminative thinking, I will cultivate openness, nondis-
crimination, and nonattachment to views in order to transform
violence, fanaticism, and dogmatism in myself and in the world.

The First Mindfulness Training reminds us to
practice protecting life and not to kill. This is a

practice that is intended to remind us of violence both small and large. As with each of the Mindfulness Trainings, it's intended not to be an absolute but a path to walk on. It isn't possible to avoid killing altogether. For example, you may say you're going to be a vegetarian so that you're less involved in the death of animals, but when you cook your vegetables to eat, many microorganisms die. So even your vegetarian diet isn't entirely vegetarian. That's okay. You're working toward less suffering. It's not that there's no suffering. But you choose the way to minimize the suffering. We can reduce the suffering a little bit every time we act, every time we eat, every day.

In a world in which people use violence in the name of idealism, religion, or God, the First Mindfulness Training helps us transform our craving, anger, and ignorance. The Second Noble Truth reminds us that our suffering will continue as long as we hold wrong views. Our craving and anger arise from ignorance, so, with Right View, we're no longer able to justify violence, and by practicing nonviolence we save and protect life, the First Mindfulness Training.

When we practice the First Mindfulness Training, we strengthen our eyes of interbeing. Our look has to be wide and open so that we can see without being caught in ideologies and dogmas. We can see that when we kill someone we kill ourselves. When we meet someone we think of as an enemy, we tend to think that we need to protect ourselves, and that hurting the other person will help keep us safe. But hurting another person doesn't keep us safe. We may think the only way to be safe is to attack the other person. But hurting or killing the person we think of as our enemy will only make more enemies. We have to understand our own anger and suffering and help the person we think of as our enemy to alleviate his or her own suffering. Violence can't end suffering. Only understanding and love can transform suffering.

In 2007, I returned to Vietnam after many years in exile. We organized a series of memorial and offering ceremonies for the seven million Vietnamese people who died in the war with the United States. In that ceremony, we made this vow: "Before our spiritual and blood ancestors, we vow that from today onward we shall never allow another ideological war to take place." The war that happened in Vietnam was an ideological war. The communist and capitalist ideologies are not Vietnamese ideologies, just like the weapons that we used to kill each other on behalf of these ideologies were not Vietnamese.

In the spring of 2013, I visited South Korea. I gave a talk there about peace between South Korea and North Korea in which I proposed that it's not enough to limit the development of a nuclear weapons program. We have to address the large amount of fear we have inside us. If there's no fear, anger, or suspicion, then people aren't going to use nuclear or any other kind of weapons. It's not the absence of nuclear weapons alone that guarantees that two countries can reconcile and have peace. It's by removing fear, anger, and suspicion that we can make true peace possible.

When you attempt to make nuclear weapons, it's not truly because you want to destroy the other side, it's because you're fearful that they will attack you first. If you want to offer help anywhere in the world, whether it's in the United States, North and South Korea, the Middle East, or anywhere, you can help to work on removing the fear, anger, and suspicion on both sides. Israelis and Palestinians, for example, both have the desire to survive as a nation and a people. Both are fearful that the other side will destroy them. Both are suspicious, because in the past what they've received from the other side has been violence. So to make true peace possible, you have to try to remove the fear, anger, and suspicion. It's not just up to politicians. Can each of us act in such a way that we can lessen the huge amount of fear, anger, and suspicion that exists?

In the spring of 2013 in Newtown, Connecticut, a young man walked into a school and started shooting at children and teachers. Many people were killed. After the event, some politicians tried unsuccessfully to pass laws that would limit the types of guns that are sold and tried to strengthen the laws restricting gun purchases as well as the safety regulations governing their use. Although such laws might have been helpful, they still don't address the underlying issues, which are people's suffering, violence, anger, and mental illness. Many people buy guns because they're afraid and they want to protect themselves. So the main, driving issue isn't nuclear weapons or guns, it's fear.

In a relationship, if reconciliation seems to be difficult, it's usually not because the two people aren't willing to reconcile, it's because the amount of anger, fear, and suspicion in each person is already too big. We often say that it's the other person's fault; we want to reconcile, but they don't. But that's rarely the case. The other person may want to reconcile, but she or he still has a lot of anger, fear, and suspicion. Telling this to the other person won't help. If you want to help someone reduce their fear, anger, and suspicion, you first have to practice to reduce the amount of fear, anger, and suspicion in yourself.

Prayer or good intention is not enough to change an angry or violent situation. The First Mindfulness Training is a reminder that you have to practice, to train yourself to lessen violence through understanding. You can do this by practicing mindfulness. Practicing mindfulness means that instead of reacting to whatever stimulus is around us or provokes us, we go back to our breathing, we calm our body, we stop our thinking, and we bring the mind home to the body in the present moment. We become more aware of our motivations, our thoughts, our actions and their consequences, and the way we speak to others. We understand ourselves better. We see our part in the situation and we see that we may be harboring misperceptions about the other person or group. With this clearer view, we see that the others are human beings like us with very much the same feelings, motivations, and concerns.

Unless we have the practice of understanding and compassion, even if we try to help in a situation in which there's tension, we may not succeed. Suppose South Korea sends North Korea a large shipment of grain and other foods, saying that the North needs a lot of food for the poor people to survive. South Korea may be motivated by the good intention to prevent starvation in the North, but the North may see it as an attempt to discredit them, as though the South were saying that the North isn't capable of feeding its own population.

Anything you do or say can be distorted and create more anger, fear, and suspicion. Our political leaders haven't been trained in the art of helping to remove fear, anger, and suspicion. That is why we have to call for help from those of us who practice compassion and deep listening and who have had some success in transforming the fear, anger, and suspicion in ourselves.

We can use the First Mindfulness Training as a reminder to continue our practice of the Fourth Mindfulness Training (deep listening and loving speech) in order to reduce fear, anger and suspicion. If we do that as a big community, our insight will grow and that will bring more peace to the world.

THE FIRST MINDFULNESS TRAINING:
CONCRETE PRACTICES

....

1 :: Walking Meditation to Take Care of Our Own Seeds of Violence, Fear, and Discrimination
We all have the seeds of violence, hatred, and discrimination in the depths of our consciousness and when these seeds are watered we suffer and can make others suffer. If someone says or does something that makes us feel hurt or afraid we need to take very good care of ourselves, and walking in mindfulness is one of the best ways to take care of

the body and mind. As we walk we recognize: "Now the seed of violence is manifesting in me." Then we recognize how much we are suffering in this moment. Still, mindfulness is there, helping us to hold the suffering and not be overwhelmed by it. This is the practice of the First Noble Truth. Then, after we have walked slowly and peacefully we begin to feel compassion for ourselves. We feel compassion because we have understood how much we are suffering. With the presence of compassion and mindfulness, we have a chance to look deeply into our suffering and see its roots. This is the practice of the Second Noble Truth. We may recognize that it is not only our suffering but the suffering of our ancestors and of the collective consciousness. This is the practice of Right View, Right Thinking, and the Noble Eightfold Path, which diminishes the suffering and helps us glimpse the Third Truth, which is the transformation of suffering into happiness. Now we're not likely to say or do anything that will hurt someone else. Our mindful steps are a wonderful way to help us transform our state of mind from a violent one into a nonviolent one.

The mind tends to dart from one thing to

another, like a monkey swinging from branch to branch without stopping to rest. Our mind has millions of pathways, and it forever pulls us back to our feeling of having been hurt and wanting to hurt in return. If we can transform our walking path into a place for meditation, our feet will take every step in full awareness. Our breathing will be in harmony with our steps, and our mind will naturally be at ease. Every step we take will cause a stream of calming energy to flow through us.

We can go back to the Earth as we walk. The Earth is our mother and a solid place of refuge. When we feel overwhelmed by hatred or anger and we want to do harm to ourselves or to others we should walk on Mother Earth and ask her to receive and embrace all our negative energy. We feel her solid, nondiscriminating presence under our feet. She is willing to receive everything—beautiful and sweet-smelling things but also whatever is foul-smelling and impure. She can receive our negative thoughts and feelings and transform them into flowers. Breathing in, we say to ourselves: "Mother Earth." Breathing out, we say to ourselves: "I come back." When we are away from

Mother Nature for too long, we get sick. Each step we take in walking meditation allows us to touch our mother, so that we can be well again. A lot of harm has been done to Mother Earth, so now it's time to kiss the Earth with our feet and heal our mother.

When we have mastered the art of mindful walking and felt its real benefits in our life we can share the practice with others. If we are a teacher or a psychotherapist we can help our students or our clients to walk in such a way that it helps them transform their strong emotions.

Many young people commit suicide because they can see no way out of the suffering that comes with strong emotions. It's wonderful if those of us who know how to walk mindfully and peacefully can share this practice with others.

When you begin to practice walking meditation, you might feel unbalanced, like a baby taking her first steps. Follow your breathing, dwell mindfully in your steps, and soon you will find your balance. Visualize a tiger walking slowly, and you will find that your steps become as majestic as hers.

You may like to start by practicing walking

meditation in the morning, allowing the energy of the pure morning air to enter you. Your movements will become smooth and your mind will become alert. Throughout the day, you will find you have a heightened awareness of your actions. When you make decisions after walking meditation, you will find that you are more calm and clear, and have more insight and compassion. With each peaceful step you take, all beings near and far will benefit.

As you walk, pay attention to each step you make. Walk slowly. Don't rush. Each step brings you into the best moment of your life. In walking meditation, you practice being aware of the number of steps you make with each breath. Notice each breath and how many steps you take as you breathe in and breathe out. In walking meditation we match our steps to our breath, and not the other way around. When you breathe in, take two or three steps, depending on the capacity of your lungs. If your lungs want two steps while breathing in, then take two steps. If you feel better with three steps, then give yourself three steps. When you breathe out, also listen to your lungs. Know how many steps your lungs want you to make while breathing out.

Our in-breath is usually shorter than our out-breath. So, you might start your practice with two steps for the in-breath and three for the out-breath: 2–3, 2–3, 2–3; or 3–4, 3–4, 3–4. As we continue, our breathing naturally becomes slower and more relaxed. If you feel you need to make one more step while breathing in, then allow yourself to enjoy that. Whenever you feel that you want to make one more step while breathing out, then allow yourself to have one more step breathing out. Every step should be enjoyable.

Don't try to control your breathing. Allow your lungs as much time and air as they need, and simply notice how many steps you take as your lungs fill up and how many you take as they empty, being mindful of both your breath and your steps. The link is the counting.

Always follow the needs of your lungs. Don't forget to practice smiling. Your half smile will bring calm and delight to your steps and your breath, and help sustain your attention. After practicing for half an hour or an hour, you will find that your breath, your steps, your counting, and your half smile come together easily. Your lungs will be healthier, and your blood will circulate better. Your way of breathing will have been transformed.

We can practice walking meditation by counting steps or by using words that support our transformation. You can create the words that are appropriate to your situation and that feel to be in rhythm with your steps and breath. Here is one example:

Aware of my emotions (breathing in)
Taking care (breathing out)
Mother Earth (breathing in)
Holding my pain (breathing out)

Every day, you walk somewhere. So adding walking meditation to your life doesn't take a lot of additional time or require you to go anywhere different. Choose a place—a staircase, your driveway, or the distance from one tree to another—to do walking meditation every day. Every path can be a walking meditation path.

2 :: Sharing the Practice

The town or locality where you live may already have a local Sangha with members who practice the Five Mindfulness Trainings.[1] But, if not, find at least one other person, more if possible, who would like to join you in the practice. You can meet up with the Sangha or your friends according to whatever schedule works for all of you, and each person can share their experience of how they practice the Mindfulness Trainings. Learning ways to protect life and stopping others from killing is something we can do most successfully as a collective. We can discuss what we can do together to prevent more violence. It may be making a commitment to talk to others, or peaceful protesting, or writing love letters to our newspaper and government representatives. It may be through theater or it may be through personal practice of nonviolence. There are many creative and effective ways that we can contribute to a safer and more peaceful world. We are more likely to discover these ways if we practice and share together.

---

[1] See iamhome.org for a list of Sanghas worldwide.

The Second Mindfulness Training reminds us to live simply and treat the environment with care.

CHAPTER 4

The Second Mindfulness Training: True Happiness GENEROSITY

Aware of the suffering caused by exploitation, social injustice, stealing, and oppression, I am committed to practicing generosity in my thinking, speaking, and acting. I am determined not to steal and not to possess anything that should belong to others; and I will share my time, energy, and material resources with those who are in need. I will practice looking deeply to see that the happiness and suffering of others are not separate from my own happiness and suffering; that true happiness is not possible without understanding and compassion; and that running after wealth, fame, power, and sensual pleasures can bring much suffering and despair. I am aware that happiness depends on my mental attitude and not on external conditions, and that I can live happily in the present moment simply by remembering that I already have more than enough conditions to be happy. I am committed to practicing Right Livelihood so that I can help reduce the suffering of living beings on Earth and reverse the process of global warming.

The Second Mindfulness Training is about taking only what is freely given and treating the environment with care. It is about learning to share material goods, time, and energy with those who are in need. The aim of this training is to end craving. Because of our craving for natural resources, because of the craving of the market for us to consume its goods, governments don't hesitate to bring an army to invade another country and end countless lives. Because of this craving, we allow poverty and hunger to exist, afraid we won't have enough for ourselves if everyone has what they need. Craving leads to the destruction of the environment and the pollution of water, the soil, and the air.

To see the connection between ourselves and other people is part of the practice of the Second Mindfulness Training. The people that we take things from are not other than ourselves. When, in the richer countries of Europe and in the United States, we forget about the suffering brought about by poverty in other parts of the world or even for people in our own country, we consume in a way that exploits poor people. Poverty creates violence, and sooner or later that violence will bring about suffering for the richer countries and the richer people. The suffering of the poor is directly related to the suffering of the rich.

Moreover, being rich does not mean being happy. Happiness is only possible when there is peace of mind, and peace of mind isn't possible without understanding and love. Many people think that happiness comes from money, fame, and sensual pleasures. But this isn't correct. People who have an abundance of these things may suffer a great deal and some of them even take their own lives because they don't have the capacity to understand and to love. If we know the teaching about how to live happily in the present moment, if we know how to make use of mindfulness to go home to the present moment, we realize that there are so many conditions of happiness that are already there. You don't need to run into the future to get more conditions. If we're happy living in the present moment, we don't have to be so afraid that our fear drives us to accumulate more wealth and power.

Each of us has an idea about happiness. We think that we have to obtain this or get rid of that before we can be truly happy. We have many ideas such as, "I really want that diploma," or "If only I had that position." We have an idea about what will make us happy. Sometimes a whole nation might embrace a certain political or ideological path, thinking it is the only way to happiness.

If you haven't been able to be happy, maybe it's because you're holding firmly to your idea of happiness. Release that idea, and happiness can come more easily. Imagine that there are many doors that open to happiness. If you open every door, then happiness has many ways to come to you. But the situation is that you have closed all the doors except one, and that is why happiness can't come. So don't close any doors. Open all the doors. Don't just commit yourself to one idea of happiness. Release the idea of happiness that you have, and then happiness can come today. Many of us are caught in an idea about how we can truly be happy. To be a good practitioner, sit down and reexamine your idea of happiness.

Many of us are attached to a number of things that we think are crucial for our well-being. Although we may have suffered a lot because of them, we're afraid to release these things to which we're attached. We may be attached to a person, a material thing, or a position in society. We think that without that one thing, we won't be safe. We need to have the insight that will give us the courage to release this attachment so we can finally be free. Joy and happiness can be born from releasing, from letting go of our ideas and attachments.

Gandhi expressed the same idea in this way: "Our ancestors knew how to stop in order to practice contentment; they did not indulge themselves without restraint and did not drown in the enjoyment of sensual pleasures. They saw that happiness depends on our way of seeing things. If our mind has love and understanding we shall have happiness. It is not necessarily true that because someone is rich that he is happy, or when he is poor he suffers." Those who live a simple life have contentment. Although they may not have a large salary, they can smile all day long and offer love every day.

The Second Mindfulness Training is also about seeing our deep connection with the Earth. We tend to see the Earth as something different from ourselves, something for us to use, to exploit or, at best, to protect. With Right View and the insight of interbeing, we see that we are made up of Earth elements such as water and minerals, and of particles that come from the solar system. The Earth is not separate from us. When we exploit and destroy the environment we harm ourselves, our descendants, and other species. By polluting the water, the soil, and the atmosphere, we pollute ourselves. If we recognize that we come from the Earth and are part of the Earth, then we will feel love and gratitude for the Earth and will naturally treat her with care and respect.

We can use the Second Mindfulness Training as a reminder to practice gratitude to our ancestors, teachers, friends, all beings, and the Earth. Our ancestors are not only human beings. We humans have come from the other animal, plant, and mineral species. Humans are very new inhabitants of this planet Earth, so we are very grateful to all the species who have inhabited this Earth much longer than we have. In China and Vietnam, we have the expression "gratitude to the heavens that cover us and to the Earth that carries us." We owe gratitude to everything around us. When we see the water coming from the tap we can be aware that water comes from mountain sources and from deep in the Earth. We can say, "Water flows wonderfully for us and our gratitude is overflowing." We are grateful to the air, to the warmth of the sun until our feeling of gratitude becomes as vast as the universe itself.

In the United States, on Thanksgiving Day, people decorate their homes and gardens with pumpkins, squash, and ears of corn. These are the fruits of the Earth. Every day we eat and receive the fruits of the Earth. We can practice gratitude for all species every minute of our waking life. True gratitude is a feeling that has no limits. We generally think of our parents as the ones who brought us up and nourished us to maturity but many other species contributed to our nourishment and growth. The sun and the Earth nourished us. The objects of our gratitude and we ourselves are one.

THE SECOND MINDFULNESS TRAINING:

CONCRETE PRACTICES

....

1 :: Remembering the Conditions of Happiness

Find a quiet spot. It could be the foot of a tree, a grassy bank, or just a quiet corner in your home. On a piece of paper write down the conditions you have to be happy. Following your breathing, come back to yourself. See all the wonderful things that your body, mind, and environment have to offer. If you have eyes that can see, that's already a huge condition for happiness. You only have to open your eyes and all the wonderful forms and colors of life appear. If you have ears that can hear, you're able to listen to the singing of the birds and the sighing of the wind in the pine trees. To have time to sit and enjoy your breathing, to have a spiritual path, to hug your loved ones, your children, your grandchildren, to have healthy food to eat: there are so many conditions for your happiness that you could cover far more than one sheet of paper in recounting them. Let go of the idea that only the future can bring you happiness. You can be happy with what you have now.

2 :: Shopping Meditation

It is possible to go shopping and not to buy anything. There was a time in Plum Village when we needed some nails. I told the children visiting us that we were going shopping. Our intention was to buy the nails and not buy anything else. However, we could look at any of the items for sale in the supermarket in order to learn about them, where they came from, and to meditate on the suffering that may have resulted from their production. For instance, if an item seemed to be very cheap we could ask ourselves whether the worker who produced it was paid a fair price. Was the method of farming sustainable? We can educate ourselves and our children by shopping mindfully and sharing afterward what we learned. The supermarket does its best to persuade us to buy things we never intended to buy, and shopping meditation helps us to be content with what we truly need. Before shopping make a list of what you need and only buy what is on the list. What makes us truly happy can't be found in the marketplace.

The Third Mindfulness Training reminds us that respect and understanding are the foundation of true love.

CHAPTER 5

The Third Mindfulness Training:
True Love   KINDNESS, LOVING

*Aware of the suffering caused by sexual misconduct, I am com-
mitted to cultivating responsibility and learning ways to protect
the safety and integrity of individuals, couples, families, and
society. Knowing that sexual desire is not love, and that sexual
activity motivated by craving always harms myself as well as
others, I am determined not to engage in sexual relations without
true love and a deep, long-term commitment made known to my
family and friends. I will do everything in my power to protect
children from sexual abuse and to prevent couples and families
from being broken by sexual misconduct. Seeing that body and
mind are one, I am committed to learning appropriate ways to
take care of my sexual energy and to cultivating loving kindness,
compassion, joy, and inclusiveness—which are the four basic
elements of true love—for my greater happiness and the greater*

happiness of others. Practicing true love, we know that we will continue beautifully into the future.

The Third Mindfulness Training is about learning how to practice true love. Many songs have lyrics that say, "I love you; I need you," as if loving means simply using another person to fulfill your need. We are taught to think that love is the feeling you have when you think you can't survive without the other person.

Our original desire as a newborn was to survive. As a tender baby who was just born, you were helpless. You had arms and feet, but you couldn't move, you couldn't go anywhere or do anything for yourself. During your birth you experienced moments of danger. Then they cut the umbilical cord. You came from a very soft, dark, and comfortable place out into bright lights and onto a hard surface. You had to expel liquid from your lungs so you could breathe your first breath—it was a dangerous moment. You didn't yet know the language of humans.

When you were just a few days old, every time you heard the sound of footsteps coming close, you were happy, because it meant that someone was bringing you milk, comfort, and warmth. You needed another person; you couldn't survive without someone being there. That is the original need, the original love, and the original fear—the fear that no one will be there to take care of you. You're completely helpless. You need another person. Hopefully, there was an adult who took care of you. Maybe it was a mother, a father, or another relative. Whoever it was, as an infant you probably fell in love with that person, their smell, the sound of their footsteps, and the shape of their face. That person is your original love, a love born from your need.

In Asia, when people kiss each other they use the nose more than the mouth. Using the nose, we can recognize the person; it's so pleasant. When we are infants, the smell of the person taking care of us is the most wonderful smell in the world, because we need that person. So in Asia, when they kiss, they mostly use their nose in order to enjoy the smell of the other person. That is the continuation of the original desire, the desire to have that person close to us, the desire to hear those steps coming closer and closer. All day and night, as an infant, we hope to hear the sound of footsteps and to be able to smell that smell.

But from this original desire of the tender infant in us may come a lot of unhealthy craving. We may feel incomplete without a partner or feel lost without a romantic relationship. We think that we need someone to protect us and take care of us, and that it's the role of the other person to do this. Perhaps being around the other person makes us feel relaxed and safe, as we did when we were taken care of as infants.

The Third Mindfulness Training is a reminder that we can love people from a place of understanding and compassion, not just out of need. When we love someone, we have to see that we are one with that person. Their suffering is our suffering and our suffering is theirs. We can't exclude the other person from our own happiness and suffering. The safety and integrity of the other person is our own safety and integrity. The body and mind of our loved one is a sacred space that needs to be respected. Only then can there be true love.

If you look at the other person's body as a tool

to satisfy your desire then the relationship loses all its sacredness. Body and mind are not two separate things. If the body is polluted, the mind is also polluted, wounded, and weighed down. If the mind is whole, the body is also whole. If we don't see the body as sacred, we won't see the mind as sacred. We should look upon guarding our body as we look upon guarding our mind and vice versa. Generally, we only share the deepest secrets of our heart with someone in whom we have complete trust, our closest lifelong friend. The same is true of our body. It's only when we have a deep and committed relationship with someone that we should entrust our body to them. In that way sexual love becomes something very sacred.

Love is a process of discovery. The Third Mindfulness Training reminds us that when we seek empty pleasure through sexual activity, we destroy happiness and we destroy love. Ill-considered sexual relations without true love make people feel they have lost something very precious in their lives. A boy or girl who is sexually abused suffers terribly, and the suffering can stay with them for the whole of their lives. Our body has certain sacred areas, which no one has the right to touch without our explicit permission, given as an adult. The wholeness of our body is linked to the wholeness of our soul. Someone who doesn't respect your body cannot respect your mind. Your body isn't a toy for someone to play with. When we guard our body, we do this also for the sake of our children, our grandchildren, and all our ancestors and descendants.

Everyone has sexual energy. Sexual energy in itself is not unwholesome. When sexual energy leads to activity that causes suffering, it is unwholesome. The Third Mindfulness Training reminds us to commit to learn ways of taking care of the sexual energy in ourselves. Of course the Buddha had sexual energy too. He became enlightened at thirty-five, a young age when sexual energy is still strong. But with his practice of mindfulness and concentration he could transform and focus this energy in other ways. He knew how to direct his energy into helping others and the world.

Eating in moderation, refraining from drinking alcohol, and ensuring that we do physical activity each day are things we can do to help ourselves take care of our sexual energy.

In my monastic tradition, we have a practice called the Second Body. We always have another monk or nun alongside us to protect us. We don't go out alone or have clandestine conversations. People who live out in the world can be constantly exposed to messages, from advertising and media sources, encouraging the expression of sexual energy. There's a great deal of sex to be found out in the world, but not much love. The focus on sexuality is so pervasive that reading the Third Mindfulness Training isn't enough. We need to learn to take care of our bodies and minds and to treat our own and others' bodies and minds with respect.

We can practice to increase our loving kindness (*maitri*), compassion (*karuna*), joy (*mudita*), and inclusiveness (*upeksha*). These are the four elements of true love that can help our own happiness and the happiness of others to grow.

Maitri, loving kindness, is the first element of true love. Maitri has the same Sanskrit root as *mitra*, which means friend. Love, at its base, is deep friendship. A friendship needs to bring about happiness. Otherwise, what's the use of having a friendship? To be a friend means to offer happiness. So if love isn't creating more happiness, if it's making you cry all the time, that's not maitri; it's the opposite.

You also need to treat yourself with loving kindness and learn to love yourself. Self-love is the foundation for loving another person. If you aren't able to love yourself and offer yourself happiness, how can you love and offer happiness to another person? When you can live in a way that brings you joy and happiness, then you'll be able to offer joy and happiness to others.

Karuna, compassion, is the second element of true love. But the word "compassion" doesn't perfectly reflect karuna. The prefix "com" means together and "passion" means to suffer. Therefore to be compassionate literally means to suffer together with the other person. But practicing karuna doesn't mean that you have to suffer. Karuna is the capacity to relieve suffering, whether that is the suffering in yourself or in the other person. You have that capacity.

When you love someone and you see them suffering, you're motivated to try to alleviate that suffering. But if you don't know how to handle the suffering in yourself, you won't be able to help the other person handle their suffering. Whenever you have a painful feeling, mindfulness of compassion (maintaining your compassion alive) can help you learn to be there for that feeling without fighting it. Then you can embrace and accept it. If you continue to practice mindful breathing, and tenderly hold your pain and sorrow, you'll be able to look deeply into your suffering and begin to understand its nature and causes. With that understanding, you can get some relief and finally you can liberate yourself from your pain and sorrow. Compassion is born from understanding. When you feel compassion for yourself, you'll be able to understand and feel compassion for others and help ease their suffering.

Suppose you're a doctor. A doctor should have compassion—hopefully! If you were a doctor and a patient would come to you full of fear and complaining of pain, even if you're a good doctor, you don't have to suffer with your patient in order to be kind and to help them. Practicing true love, you don't have to suffer with your beloved. Instead, you help both yourself and the other person to suffer less.

Mudita, joy, is the third element of true love. Mindful awareness means you have access to feelings of joy and happiness at any moment. You don't need money. You don't need to go to the shopping center. If you know the art of releasing, the art of mindfulness, the art of concentration, the art of insight, then you can bring a feeling of joy and happiness at any time.

There are ways you can bring joy to yourself. If you know how to bring joy to yourself, then you'll know how to bring joy to others. If you're truly joyful and your joy has wholesome roots, then it benefits other people. Although you haven't done anything, just because you are inhabited by joy, we gain happiness from being around you.

Just letting go can bring joy and happiness. There are attachments and ideas we can release. We can let go of stories from the past, which we keep telling ourselves, and of old habitual ways of thinking. Releasing, letting go, can sound simple, but it's an art. Sitting and breathing, we can focus on releasing our stories so we can cultivate our own happiness. When we practice correctly we experience joy straightaway.

The fourth element of true love is **upeksha**, inclusiveness. Upeksha is often translated as equanimity, but I prefer to think of it as inclusiveness. In true love, you don't exclude anyone. This is the foundation of true love. In true love there's no longer any discrimination. Happiness is no longer an individual matter. Suffering, too, is no longer an individual matter. You and the other person are the same person. His suffering is your own suffering; his happiness is your own happiness; your joy is his joy. There's no longer any barrier, any frontier, between the lover and the one who is loved. In that sense there's no longer any separate self.

If you're caught by your attachment to your beloved one and cut off from all other people and species, then that's not true love. If your love is true love, it will benefit everyone, not only humans, but also animals, plants, and minerals. To love one person is an opportunity for you to love everyone and all species. If you're going in a good direction with your love, it will grow more inclusive all the time. True love is generated from within. With true love you feel complete in yourself; you don't need something from outside to make you feel whole. True love is like the shining sun. The sun is sufficient in itself. It offers light to everyone. It doesn't say, "I only want to offer light to this one person." It doesn't exclude anyone.

SEX IS NOT LOVE

Sex is an instinct of preservation and it can feel very pleasurable, but that is something very different from love. Every living being wants to continue into the future, not only humans but animals and plants as well. Plants produce seeds so they can continue into the future. Having a desire to reproduce is a very natural thing. Other species also have sex for pleasure and not just for procreation, but that doesn't make it love. Sex is something natural, with humans, with animals, and with plants. We shouldn't be against sex. But we shouldn't confuse it with love.

It's possible for us to cultivate the four elements of true love through the practices of releasing, being mindful, being concentrated, and looking deeply to get the insight we need. Spending time each day with each of these practices can help us handle the suffering inside and transform it into peace and joy. That is already love. You don't need another person in order to practice love. You practice love on yourself first. And when you succeed, loving another person becomes something very natural. It's like a lamp that shines and makes many people happy. Your presence in the world becomes very important, because your presence is the presence of love.

THE THIRD MINDFULNESS TRAINING:
CONCRETE PRACTICES

....

1 :: A Mindful Diet

The Third Mindfulness training reminds us that it's sometimes necessary to take care of our sexual energy. Sexual energy is not just produced by the body but also by the mind. When we consume the Internet, video games, or other media unskillfully we can arouse sexual energy in our mind in a way that is completely disassociated from love.

Advertisements can play into our sexual energy without us even noticing. When we feel that our sexual energy is too strong and could lead us to do things that will cause suffering, we need to look carefully at what we are consuming, both in terms of media and entertainment, and in terms of edible food. Changing our diet, eating healthier food, eating less, and not eating late at night, we can focus on what our bodies need and shift our physical focus more inward.

2 :: Physical Exercise

Physical exercise is a wonderful way of taking care of sexual energy. Exercise your body every day, even if it's just in small ways, a walk around the block or ten minutes of stretching. There are forms of exercise, including qigong and yoga, that are specifically designed to help channel sexual energy, but committing to physical exercise in almost any form will help your body and mind channel sexual energy in a way that is nourishing and healthy.

3 :: Metta Meditation

Metta means loving kindness. Practicing this meditation helps facilitate our access to compassion and true love. To practice this love meditation, sit still, calm your body and your breathing, and contemplate by using the verses below:

May I be peaceful, happy, and light in body and spirit.
May I be safe and free from injury.
May I be free from anger, afflictions, fear, and anxiety.

May I learn to look at myself with the eyes of understanding
*   and love.*
May I recognize and be in touch with the seeds of happiness
*   within myself.*
May I identify and embrace the sources of suffering in myself.

May I nourish the seeds of joy in myself every day.
May I live fresh, solid, and free.
May I be free from attachment and aversion but not
*   be indifferent.*

The sitting position is a wonderful position for practicing this exercise. Sitting still, you are not too preoccupied with other matters, so you can look deeply at yourself as you are and cultivate love for yourself.

Begin with yourself first. Later on you can use the same exercise to cultivate love for others, by replacing the words "May I" with: "May he/she/they be peaceful, happy, and light, etc."

You know how much you want these things for yourself and for others.

After you've meditated to feel true love for yourself, you know you have the capacity to realize these aspirations because you've experienced them to a greater or lesser degree. Then you can do the same meditation on someone else, first of all a friend or a dear one, then someone you feel neutral about, and then someone you dislike, and then someone you love very much and to whom you may feel a strong attachment. If you're successful you'll develop equanimity and be able to love and understand even the person you formerly disliked. You may also see the person you love in a different light with more understanding and fewer wrong perceptions. You'll see the difficulties of that person. You may also see their shortcomings more clearly, but you'll also have the capacity to accept them.

May you be peaceful, happy, and light in body and spirit.
May you be safe and free from injury.
May you be free from anger, afflictions, fear, and anxiety.

May you learn to look at yourself with the eyes of
understanding and love.
May you recognize and be in touch with the seeds of
happiness within you.
May you identify and embrace the sources of suffering
in yourself.

May you nourish the seeds of joy in yourself every day.
May you live fresh, solid, and free.
May you be free from attachment and aversion, but not
be indifferent.

The Fourth Mindfulness Training reminds us that harmonious relationships are based on loving communication.

CHAPTER 6

The Fourth Mindfulness Training:
Deep Listening and Loving Speech

Aware of the suffering caused by unmindful speech and the inability to listen to others, I am committed to cultivating loving speech and compassionate listening in order to relieve suffering and to promote reconciliation and peace in myself and among other people, ethnic and religious groups, and nations. Knowing that words can create happiness or suffering, I am committed to speaking truthfully, using words that inspire confidence, joy, and hope. When anger is manifesting in me, I am determined not to speak. I will practice mindful breathing and walking in order to recognize and to look deeply into my anger. I know that the roots of anger can be found in my wrong perceptions and lack of understanding of the suffering in myself and in the other person. I will speak and listen in a way that can help myself and the other person to transform suffering and see the way out of difficult situations. I am determined not to spread news that I do not know to be certain and not to utter words that can cause division or discord. I will practice Right Diligence to nourish my capacity for understanding, love, joy, and inclusiveness, and gradually transform anger, violence, and fear that lie deep in my consciousness.

The Third Mindfulness Training, which helps us practice love and understanding for others and ourselves, is the basis for practicing loving speech and deep listening. Often, our anger and irritation get in the way of our being able to use loving speech, and we speak in a way that causes harm to our family, community, and coworkers.

The Fourth Mindfulness Training focuses on Right Speech and deep listening because we can only understand another person when we're able to truly listen to them. When we can listen to others with deep compassion, we can understand their pain and difficulties. This helps us feel calm and receptive and it's easy for us to talk with them using loving speech. Loving speech is an essential tool when we want to build a community that's a healing and loving refuge for people.

It's helpful if, before speaking, you've practiced being able to listen well. You can begin to practice this on your own by listening to yourself in your meditation. Listening deeply to another is also a form of meditation. We follow our breathing and practice concentration and we learn things about the other person that we never knew before. When we practice deep listening, we can help the person we're listening to remove the perceptions that are making her suffer. We can restore harmony in our partnerships, our friendships, our family, our community, our nation, and between nations. It is that powerful.

Sometimes when we attempt to listen to another person, we can't hear them because we haven't listened to ourselves. Our own strong emotions and thoughts are so loud in us, crying out for our attention, that we can't hear the other person. We think that what they're saying only confirms or contradicts our own thoughts and emotions. Therefore before we listen to another, we need to spend time listening to ourselves. We can sit with ourselves, come home to ourselves, and listen to what emotions rise up, without judging or interrupting them. We can listen to whatever thoughts come up as well, and then let them pass without holding on to them. Then, when we've spent some time listening to ourselves, we can listen to those around us.

When you practice compassionate listening, it's important to remember that you listen with only one purpose, and that is to help the other person to suffer less. You give the other person a chance to say what is in his heart. Even if the other person says something harsh, provocative, or incorrect, you still continue to listen with compassion.

You're able to do that because as you sit and listen you are practicing mindfulness of compassion. During the whole time of listening, you practice mindful breathing and remind yourself, "I am listening to him with only one purpose, to give him a chance to empty his heart and to suffer less. I may be the first person who has listened to him like this. If I were to interrupt him and correct him, that would transform the session into a debate and I would fail in my practice. Even if there are misperceptions and wrong information in what he says, I'm not going to interrupt him and correct him. In a few days I may offer him some information to help him correct his perceptions, but not now."

If you can maintain this mindfulness of compassion alive in your heart during the time of listening, then you're protected by the energy of compassion, and what the other person says won't touch off the energy of irritation and anger in you. In that way, you can listen for an hour or more, and the quality of your listening will help the other person to suffer less.

When people listen to each other like that, they truly recognize the humanity and the suffering of the other person. You see the other person is a human being, someone very much like yourself. You no longer look at that person with suspicion, anger, or fear. And when it's your turn to speak, you can easily practice using loving speech.

After listening to the other, and only at a time when that person is ready to listen, we can practice loving speech. Loving speech is not something we only use in a relationship or with close family and friends. You can practice loving speech every time you speak.

So much harm is caused by wrong speech. The First Mindfulness Training is about not causing violence and not killing. Violence can be caused by our speech, not just by our physical actions. Buddhist texts mention four kinds of wrong speech: lying; exaggerating or embellishing the truth; speaking in order to cause division; insulting and speaking badly about others. These are all forms of incorrect speech that can cause serious violence and harm.

Lying also includes twisting the truth or saying what's partially true. Exaggerating means intentionally making something out to be greater or more extreme than it was. For example if something isn't particularly beautiful you say it's tremendously ugly. We add and embellish or we invent details so that it sounds more interesting and people will want to listen, but this kind of speech can lead to misunderstanding and distrust. Divisive speech means that we talk to someone in such a way that makes him dislike someone else. Or we speak of the same thing differently to different people, in a way that creates misunderstanding.

We have to practice speaking the truth and speaking it skillfully. Otherwise, we may say something that we think is truthful but that might make others suffer or despair. Telling the truth unskill-fully is not wholesome or helpful behavior. Just because we've observed or experienced something doesn't mean we should speak about it if doing so will make others suffer. For instance, if we have to give someone some bad news, the other person may become so depressed by our news that they're unable to function. A doctor or nurse needs to be compassionate and very skillful in not creating unnecessary fear in a patient or the loved ones of a patient. If we see that someone is putting on a lot weight, we don't need to say, "You've gained a lot of weight!" This kind of speaking is not Right Speech.

When we see someone suffer because of some-thing we said, we may be tempted to say, "Well, I was only telling the truth." It may have been the truth but it was very unskillful and we should tell ourselves that we are determined to train ourselves not to tell the truth in an insensitive way. We have to tell the truth in such a way that it benefits others, the world, and ourselves. When we tell the truth, we do so with compassion; we speak in such a way that the hearer can accept what we're saying.

We can practice loving speech in our writing as

well. Many people now communicate by email and text messaging more than they do in person or on the telephone. When you write something, and the person who is reading it can't see your face or hear the tone of your voice, it's even easier for them to have a misperception. It's very important that we write with mindfulness and the intention to use loving speech, whether we're sending an email or writing an article. Journalists can help relieve the suffering in the world by using their words to write clear accounts and commentaries on what's happening in the world, using both truthful and loving speech.

Deep listening can work on a large scale, not just in relationships. After the attacks on the World Trade Center and the Pentagon in 2001, I suggested the United States organize a session of deep listening to the American people's suffering. They should invite people representing those who feel that they're victims of discrimination, violence, anger, fear, social injustice and so on, and give them a chance to speak out. If we don't understand our own suffering, fear, anger, and despair, then we can't help another country or people to do the same. Since that time I have recommended this for Europe, Africa, the Middle East, North and South Korea, and for anyplace where there's tension between two groups or two countries. There's no need to jump right into an offensive or defensive solution to every conflict. If we as a group, a region, or a country can listen to ourselves and transform, we would be more able to help remove fear, anger, and suspicion in the other group.

Using loving, gentle speech means letting go of all anger, fear, and suspicion. It's an effort to try to understand and to be understood. If you can speak with this kind of language, and if you're sincere, the other person will be able to sense your sincerity and will tell you what wrong they feel you've done to them. Then you'll be able to find out the roots of their wrong perceptions and you'll have a chance to offer them real information that they can use to correct their perceptions. If they can remove their wrong perceptions, then they can reduce their suspicion, fear, and anger. If you see that in this situation of misunderstanding you have something to apologize for, it's important to be willing to do so straight away.

Suppose a father is having difficulties with his teenage son. The son and father have both made each other suffer a lot. The son doesn't dare to get close to his father because he's afraid he'll have to suffer again. The father doesn't understand his son's fear. Instead he thinks that his son is trying to defy him or boycott him. So suspicion and wrong perceptions continue to build up every day.

If the father can see the suffering in his son—the existence of anger, fear, confusion, and suspicion—he may like to help his child. He knows that his son has suffered a lot because he doesn't know how to handle the amount of anger, fear, and suspicion he has inside. Similarly, if the son has had a chance to listen to and understand his own fear, anger and suspicion, then he's in a position to be able to help his father. When he's able to see the amount of suffering in his father, his way of looking at his father will be different. Seeing the suffering in his father, he's motivated by a desire to say something or do something to help his father suffer less.

It only takes one of them, either the father or the son, to begin to restore communication. One of them can say, "I know you have suffered so much in the last many years. I haven't been able to help you to suffer less. In fact I've reacted with anger and stubbornness and made you suffer more. It hasn't been my intention to make you suffer. It's just because I haven't been able to see or understand the suffering in you. So please tell me what's in your heart, what are your difficulties, your suffering, your fear, your anger, so that I'll be able to understand. I believe that if I can understand your suffering, I'll be more skillful, I won't say or do things to make you suffer like I have in the past. I need you to help me, because if you won't help me, who will?" That is the way we can begin to try to restore communication, whether in families, friendships, romantic relationships, or between groups of people.

Using loving speech like this isn't easy. It takes diligence. Right Diligence is the part of the Noble Eightfold Path that's closely connected with Right Speech. The first aspect of Right Diligence is that we can practice not watering the unbeneficial seeds in us. In Buddhism, we speak of all the various potential states of mind as seeds in each of us. We aren't necessarily conscious of these seeds, but we all have all the seeds within us and they contain all the different emotions, thoughts, and perceptions that we may have. We call the place where they live "store consciousness." If something triggers these seeds—for example, if someone says something unkind that waters your seed of anger—they will come up and manifest in the upper level of consciousness, mind consciousness. In mind consciousness they're called mental formations; in store consciousness they're seeds. Store consciousness is like the basement of our home. Mind consciousness is like the living room. Usually we put the things we don't like in the basement. We want our living room to be presentable.

Loving speech requires the diligence of noticing and moving away when we find that we are watering the seeds of envy, anger, or despair in our store consciousness. When there is a chance of a strong emotion arising you have to sing a lullaby to help that emotion to sleep in store consciousness. Our breathing and mindful steps can also be a soothing lullaby. Try to keep the unbeneficial things in store consciousness before they manifest because when they manifest they will make you suffer and they will be strengthened at the base. The fact is that if you allow anger to come up and occupy the whole living room, and if you allow anger to stay long, then at the base it will be strengthened and become more important. If you get angry every day, then your seed of anger will grow bigger and bigger every day, and it will be much more difficult for compassion to grow because there won't be space for it. Without room for compassion, it will be difficult to use loving speech.

If our anger, jealousy, or despair does come up, we still don't need to let it take over. We can practice walking meditation to become more calm. We can also deliberately call up the seed of compassion by thinking of those people and places that easily put us in touch with our compassion. However, we should remember that at this moment the two people who are most in need of compassion are our self and the person with whom we are angry. When we water the seed of compassion, the anger will be released back into store consciousness, and loving speech becomes possible. When that compassion arises in you, stay with it as long as possible. Don't rush to speak right away. This is part of Right Diligence, taking the time to strengthen the compassion within us.

You can think of the seeds of compassion and understanding as good friends. If a good friend has come to your living room, try your best to keep her or him with you as long as possible so that goodness will continue to grow. Next time, these good things will manifest more easily, because they've become important. Sometimes you don't have to invite them, they just come up into your living room. You can get used to happiness being there. Happiness becomes a regular thing, a normal thing. Perhaps for you right now, happiness isn't normal, it only comes around from time to time. But if we water the seeds of happiness, they will manifest by themselves more and more often without invitation. We will find that when we listen deeply to ourselves, we will be able to listen to the happiness, as well as to the suffering, and loving speech and compassionate listening will come more easily with others, creating more happiness for them as well.

THE FOURTH MINDFULNESS TRAINING:

CONCRETE PRACTICES

....

1 :: Right Thinking

If we want to practice Right Speech, we have to practice Right Thinking. Sooner or later we'll inevitably speak and act according to the way that we think. When we find ourselves thinking negatively about another person, we try to think in a more positive way. We can think of the benefits that that person has conferred on us. We can give our attention to the difficulties and hardships that that person has had to face in order to give rise to compassion. If we need help from a third person to be able to understand that person we should go to someone who can really help us to see the positive things in him and help us to understand his suffering. We don't talk to a third person in order to seek an ally to oppose him.

2 :: Not Gossiping

Gossip does a tremendous amount of damage. We can practice not to listen to gossip and not to participate in conversations during which people are gossiping about others. We can be careful not to talk negatively about someone behind their back except when our intention is to help that person out of his difficulties. If our habit energy for indulging in this kind of wrong speech is very strong, we can express regret to another every time we make the mistake of negative or unbeneficial talking behind someone's back.

3 :: The Six Mantras

The six mantras are an important practice of loving speech and they are easy to practice. During a family retreat the children always learn how to practice the six mantras and they make beautiful calligraphies of them. A mantra is a magic formula that has the power, when recited with concentration and insight, to change the situation. Often mantras are recited in Sanskrit and we don't always understand the meaning. But the six mantras can be translated into any language and we can understand their meaning straight away. Sometimes we say the mantras out loud for the other person to hear and sometimes we say them quietly to ourselves. You can also reword the mantras to fit your own needs.

1. I am here for you

Sometimes we hide ourselves in the morning news at breakfast time. Sometimes we're lost in our thinking and our plans. We're driving our car and our loved one is sitting alongside us but we have forgotten about him. He may feel ignored and lonely while we are lost in some project, anxiety, or regret. Sometimes when we're eating a meal we don't even know who's sitting alongside us. Our loved one is there physically but it's as if she's not truly there. You could ask the person who seems to be lost in her thinking: "Darling, is anyone at home?" If you're lucky she'll come back to herself and say: "Darling, I'm here for you." She won't just be saying the words, she will truly be there and you can both be happy together. To love someone you need to be there one hundred percent. The mantra "I am here for you" says a lot in very few words. It says that I care about you, I enjoy being in your presence and it helps the other person to feel supported and happy.

2. I know you are there and I am very happy

Sometimes we forget about impermanence. We

think that she will be with us forever and we forget how precious her presence is in this moment. People who are dying often regret that they didn't spend enough time with their loved ones and didn't express their feelings to their loved ones. Once we're really there for the other person, that person becomes something very real. The object of our awareness may not just be a person, it could be a magnolia tree or the moon. When the other person is real she is a wonderful manifestation of life and we need to let her know that, for her happiness and for ours. It means, "Mother, I am so happy you are alive and close to me in this moment," or, "My child, how wonderful to have a fresh, loving son like you."

3. I feel your pain and I am here for you

I, or someone else, may have said or done something to hurt the other person. If I have hurt him, I want to know about it. But I don't expect him to be able to talk about it straight away. It may still be too painful. But I do want the other person to know that I'm sensitive to his pain and that I'm ready just to sit, breathe, and be with him. When you have sat quietly together for a little while, you may like to invite the other person for a gentle walk in nature to revive and refresh the joy of being alive.

4. I suffer; please help

Sometimes this mantra is the most difficult one to practice. It takes humility to admit that you have been hurt and need help; there is the fear of rejection. Still, we have to let our loved ones know when they've hurt us, otherwise the hurt can become so great that we have to separate from each other. This mantra could mean: "Please be there to listen to what I experienced that hurt me and please explain to me why you said or did that. It's very possible that I'm suffering because of a wrong perception. But only you can clear up that wrong perception for me."

5. This is a happy moment

This mantra can be practiced at any moment. You may have just sat down to a meal together and someone can ask: "What kind of moment is this?" And someone else can reply: "This is a happy moment." We have the tendency to forget the happiness that is

available at any moment and we can remember this
happiness by saying this mantra.

6. You're partly right

This mantra helps us from falling into the com-
plexes of inferiority and superiority. Sometimes
you receive a large amount of praise. You do need
to be praised from time to time, but you want to
be careful not to become too proud because of the
praise. So you say to yourself or out loud: "You are
partly right." It means: "Yes, I do have that gift,
that talent, but it's not just mine; it has been hand-
ed down to me by my ancestors. And everyone has
talents and gifts of some kind."

Sometimes you are criticized. You do need
a certain amount of criticism in order to make
progress, but it's important not to be caught in
the criticism and become paralyzed by it. You can
say the mantra to yourself or out loud. It means:
"Yes, I do manifest that unfortunate characteristic
sometimes, but I am much more than that. This is
something that I have received from my ancestors
and am in the process of transforming it for them
and for me."

4 :: Keeping Communication Open

We are all flowers in the garden of humanity, and flowers need water in order to be able to stand up straight and flourish. Our words of appreciation for each other can be like the water. Not all flowers are the same. Some need more water than others, but all need water. Whenever someone does something to make us happy, we can let them know that they have made us happy. In some cases we can say: "That made me very happy." Some flowers like to be watered from a distance. They don't like the water to be poured directly onto their leaves but onto the ground above their roots. When we water the flower of certain people, we need to do so in a way that's not too direct and doesn't make them feel embarrassed: "I do appreciate having someone around here who knows how to sing," could be more appropriate than saying: "What a lovely voice you have." It all depends on the person. We don't speak in the same way to each person because everyone is different.

The ability to apologize sincerely and express regret for the unskillful things we say or do can relieve a great deal of suffering in the other person. Once we realize that we may have said or done something to make another suffer we should find a way to apologize as soon as possible.

When we express regret we do so unconditionally. We don't need to make excuses for our having committed the mistake. We can say: "I wasn't mindful at the time. I know that kind of language can be hurtful. Please forgive me. I don't want to say such things in the future." We don't apologize for the sake of receiving a reciprocal apology from the other person. When someone else offers us an apology, we always accept it and offer understanding and forgiveness in return.

The Fifth Mindfulness Training reminds us that mindful consumption can ease suffering and nourish body and mind.

CHAPTER 7

The Fifth Mindfulness Training:
Nourishment and Healing   INTERBEING

Aware of the suffering caused by unmindful consumption, I am committed to cultivating good health, both physical and mental, for myself, my family, and my society by practicing mindful eating, drinking, and consuming. I will practice looking deeply into how I consume the Four Kinds of Nutriments, namely edible foods, sense impressions, volition, and consciousness. I am determined not to gamble, or to use alcohol, drugs, or any other products which contain toxins, such as certain websites, electronic games, TV programs, films, magazines, books, and conversations. I will practice coming back to the present moment to be in touch with the refreshing, healing, and nourishing elements in me and around me, not letting regrets and sorrow drag me back into the past nor letting anxieties, fear, or craving pull me out of the present moment. I am determined not to try to cover up loneliness, anxiety, or other suffering by losing myself in consumption. I will contemplate interbeing and consume in a way that preserves peace, joy, and well-being in my body and consciousness and in the collective body and consciousness of my family, my society, and the Earth.

The Fifth Mindfulness Training is about mindful consumption and health. This includes the practice of dwelling happily and peacefully in the present moment. The Buddha has said that nothing can survive without food. This means that our health, our happiness, our love, our peace as well as our anger, depression, and despair need food to continue to survive. This is why we have to consume in a way that supports good health of body and mind.

In Buddhism, we talk of consuming four kinds of nutriment or food: edible food, sense impressions, volition, and consciousness. Most of us absorb many toxins because so many unhealthy and addictive things are being produced all the time, with the intention of creating more consumption. A lot of the sickness, violence, anger, and despair around us result from toxic consumption that leads to ill-being. Mindful consumption is a concrete path toward a more nourishing and healing society.

The first nutriment the Buddha talked about is edible food. Many of us eat unconsciously. We are rushing from one place to another, talking while we eat, or struggling to feed a family after a tiring day of work. Many of us get our food from a place, like the supermarket, that is very disconnected from the place where our food is grown. Every time before we eat a piece of food, it's good to practice looking deeply to see where that piece of food has come from.

Countries such as China and India used to be primarily vegetarian. Now, many people who have just gotten out of the situation of poverty in these countries want to eat meat like the rich people they see on television or read about in magazines. But the production of meat contributes to poverty and hunger by using up key farmland that could be used to grow larger amounts of other foods that could feed more people. If you continue to look deeply into eating a piece of meat, you may see the fear and frustration of the animal that has been killed. The body and mind of the animal are not separate. When the animal is very afraid, in pain, and completely unable to do anything to save her life, all that frustration and pain goes into her flesh and then the human consumer eats it. Even if we're eating a vegetarian diet, we may be eating foods that have been processed with toxic chemicals; the crops may have been picked by workers who aren't treated fairly or paid properly; the foods may be transported long distances; and there are many other ways in the growing, transporting, and marketing of crops that contribute to suffering. It's not enough to just say that we eat vegetarian or vegan food and then not think about other aspects of our food consumption. Every time we eat or go shopping, we can look deeply into the process of how the food came to our table.

Sense impression is another kind of food we eat everyday. Sensory impressions are everything we take in through our senses: eyes, ears, nose, tongue, body, and mind. Ads on billboards, conversations we overhear or take part in, videos we watch, and texts that we receive—all these things penetrate into us, whether we want them to or not.

According to the Fifth Mindfulness Training

we can see the computer as something we need to take great care in using. If we're not careful we can become addicted to going on the Internet. In our tradition, when a monk or a nun uses the Internet, she or he has to have another monk or nun alongside so that they don't get sucked into toxic consumption. While many of us use computers for work and can't apply this practice, we can make agreements in our homes and families about how we use digital media. We can agree on specific times and places where this media is used and we can agree not to use it as the default way we spend time with other people.

When you have a conversation with a friend, you consume. What the other person says may be full of jealousy, craving, or despair, and while you're listening to him or to her, you're consuming. If you don't have enough insight and compassion, these poisons will penetrate into you, and you will get sick after a number of years. We can give ourselves permission to withdraw politely from an unhealthy conversation. Whenever you've been listening to a great deal of negativity, for instance if you're a psychotherapist, you need to refresh yourself before you do anything else. A good way is to do walking meditation and be in touch with all the wonderful manifestations of life that are there in nature. In your daily life you should have enough time to consume healthy things that nourish your joy, your happiness, your compassion, and your understanding.

When you read an article in a magazine, you consume. That article may be full of anger, fear, and violence, and if you continue to read articles like that every day, you'll get sick. People who commit violent acts have always consumed a lot of violence, anger, and fear before committing that act. We are so busy that we don't have the time to protect each other.

Volition is the third source of nutriment. Volition is your aspiration, your deepest desire, what you want to do with your life. This is a very powerful source of energy that helps us to be alive. Yet many of us don't take the time to sit down and identify our deepest desires. If your deepest desire in you is to help save our planet, this is good nourishing food. If your deepest desire is to help children to be better protected, to have better education, to have a better environment, that is good food. But if your deepest desire is to have more money, fame, power, and sensual pleasure, this is toxic food that leads to craving, attachment, overwork, taking what should go to others, and other forms of living without mindfulness.

If we're motivated by compassion and a desire to help ourselves and others to suffer less, that's a much healthier and more nourishing kind of food. The energy provided by this kind of deepest desire, the ideal to serve, is very powerful and can give us a lot of strength to confront the difficulties presented to us in our daily lives. Our practice is to reexamine the food of intention that we consume every day, to make sure we're providing ourselves with good, high quality food in terms of our volition.

The fourth nutriment is consciousness. We have many good things in our consciousness like mindfulness, concentration, insight, love, compassion, and joy. If we know the practice of mindfulness, we may touch the seeds of joy, happiness, mindfulness, and wisdom in us so that they become wholesome, healthy energies; that is good consumption.

The body can also consume itself. If we go on a fast for ten or fifteen days, our bodies begin to consume the fat and toxins that have been stored. You can survive a month without eating because there is a reserve of nutrients in your body.

Our consciousness consumes our thoughts and feelings and the environments in which we spend time. We need to be aware of what we're feeding our consciousness. Consciousness can consume the good things it contains, or it can consume the things that aren't so good.

Suppose you've suffered a lot as a child. You have many sad memories of the times you suffered, and all of these are still stored in your consciousness. Many of us have made a habit of going back to the past to experience again and again the suffering that we endured in the past. It's as if we're watching a film of the past over and over again, reliving the suffering of the past. The past has become a kind of prison for us, and we're no longer free to enjoy the wonders of life available in the present moment.

There are animals that are ruminants, like water buffalo and cows. After chewing and swallowing, they bring up the food again and they chew and swallow it again. There are people who continue to consume the suffering of the past in that way. They spend their time during the day ruminating over their own suffering from the past.

The practice of mindfulness can help us get out of that prison and begin to learn how to live our lives in the present moment. If we are aware that we're replaying the past, we can make a concentrated effort to notice something that is healthy and wonderful right in front of us at that very moment. It might be a part of our body that is working well and not aching; it may be the blue sky or the softness of a pillow under our head. If we breathe and pay attention to this wonderful thing that is present with us right now, then the movie will recede and lose some of its power, as if it no longer is being fed the electricity it needs to keep going.

You can even take the hand of the wounded child within you and invite her to come with you into the present moment. This can be very nourishing and healing. It will make you stronger so that later on when you want to look into the past you can do so with more perspective, while remaining firmly grounded in the present moment. This way you don't lose yourself in the sorrows of the past.

There is also the food of collective consciousness. If you're with a group of people who are all practicing being mindful together, as a group you'll produce a collective energy of mindfulness, joy, and compassion. If, however, you're in a group or a neighborhood where people are angry, violent, fearful, and hateful, then you and everyone around you will consume this food and will begin to act, react, speak, and look like they do, and to express the energy of anger, fear, and violence, whether you want to or not. Together these individuals create a collective energy of violence, anger, and hate that you can feel every time you go to that area. If you live in a place like this, or if your children go to school in a place like this, you and your family are consuming that food. If you stay around that energy for a few years, you'll continue to consume the collective energy of hate and violence. If we can become more aware of our consumption, and deliberately focus on surrounding ourselves with people who are producing the energy of mindfulness, understanding, and love, then we can protect ourselves, our children, and our society, and get out of this present situation that's full of anger, fear, violence, and despair. When we're nourished and strong enough, we may be able to help transform that negative environment.

The Fifth Mindfulness Training is about happiness. We consume because we want to be happy. But consumption is not true happiness. People consume in order to cover up their suffering. Many people pour themselves a glass of alcohol or open the refrigerator to take something to eat or drink in order to help them forget their suffering, their difficulties, their loneliness, or their weariness with life. This is something peculiar to our modern society.

Happiness is not something that we have to look for and find somewhere else. Returning to the present moment, we are in touch with the wonders of life inside and around us. With the help of our mindful breathing and mindful steps, we can produce happiness straightaway. When we have mindfulness, concentration, and insight we become very rich people who are able to produce much happiness for ourselves and others; we don't need to run after anything anymore.

THE FIFTH MINDFULNESS TRAINING:
CONCRETE PRACTICES

....

1 :: Mindful Eating

When we eat a meal, there are two objects of our mindfulness: the food and the people who are there with us during the meal. Practicing in this way we are sure to find better and better ways of consuming food without exploiting our Earth and other living beings. Before eating a meal you can read, either aloud or to yourself, the Five Contemplations. Of course we don't just read the Contemplations but we meditate on the words throughout the meal.

The Five Contemplations

1. This food is a gift of the whole universe, the Earth, the sky, and much hard work.

2. May we eat in mindfulness and with gratitude so as to be worthy to receive it.

3. May we transform our unskillful states of mind, especially our greed.

4. May we keep our compassion alive by eating in such a way that we reduce the suffering of beings, preserve our planet, and reverse the process of global warming.
5. We accept this food in order to nourish our brotherhood and sisterhood, build our Sangha, and realize our ideal of serving all beings.

If we look deeply we shall see that the topsoil from which our vegetables grow is composed of the dead bodies of many plants and animals including humans, so we say that it is the gift of numerous living beings.

In order to be worthy of the food we have received, we simply have to be mindful and feel grateful while we're eating. If we're not mindful and grateful the food loses its reality and becomes like ghost food. When we feel grateful, we feel happy. We feel grateful to Mother Earth, to Father Sun, and to all those who have worked so hard to produce the food. Each grain of rice is soft and fragrant but it is also the result of the suffering of the little animals who died as it was cultivated and harvested as well as the suffering of the workers who harvested it. Meditating like this, we see how precious food is and we never want to waste it.

We don't need to think while we eat. In Plum Village, before we eat we sometimes remind ourselves that in the same way we normally turn off the television before we eat, let's also turn off the radio station with the call letters "NST" (nonstop thinking) so that we are truly able to enjoy the food and the presence of our family or our Sangha. Unnecessary thinking is an unskillful state of mind. Sometimes we eat our thoughts rather than the food; we're so busy thinking that we don't even know what's in our mouth. Before we put something in our mouth we can look at it for a moment and call it by its name. If it's a piece of carrot, we know that we're going to chew carrot. We can chew it as many as fifty times so that it becomes liquid and is easy to digest. While we chew like that we visualize the carrot as it grew in the field and how the rain and sunshine have come into it.

When we go shopping we're careful to buy the food that doesn't cause too much harm to our planet. If we're eating with our children, before the meal begins we can ask them to tell everyone present about one or two items on the table: where it comes from, whether it was grown organically and so on.

We eat to maintain a healthy body and mind in order to do the things that we most want to do: cultivate brotherhood and sisterhood, build Sangha, and be able to serve others. Eating food should nourish us spiritually as well as physically.

The practice of fasting can help us become healthier and more sensitive to our body's needs. Much has been written about fasting and there are many ways to do it. Each of us can find a way to fast that suits our own constitution and can help purify body and mind. Some people fast one day a week or one day a month on a regular basis and the money that they save by not eating they donate to relieve the hunger in the world. An annual fast of a longer period of time is also very helpful.

2 :: Selective Television Watching

I knew a family in the United States that was contemplating whether or not to get rid of their television. Mother, father, grandmother, and all three children sat down to discuss the matter. In the end they decided to keep the television, but with certain conditions. At the beginning of every week they would sit down together and choose the programs they were going to watch. Sometimes it wasn't easy to come to an agreement about what would be nourishing for the whole family. The parents tried not to be too strict and sometimes yielded to the children's requests even when they didn't really want to. There was one condition that was very helpful: after watching a program there would be a feedback session. Each member of the family would report on how they felt during and after watching the program—whether they felt inspired, compassionate, and that life has meaning, or whether they felt tired, frustrated, or overexcited. Everyone learned a great deal from this process and the children quickly became able to discern what kind of television watching was good for their state of mind. They no longer needed their parents to decide for them.

If our practice can be this powerful individually, imagine how powerful it could be if we practiced collectively.

CHAPTER 8

A Global Ethic

In 1993, at the Parliament of World Religions Conference held in Chicago, there was a summit conference on global ethics. During the congress the Swiss theologian Hans Küng presented a declaration toward a global ethic. In this declaration, Dr. Küng encouraged all religions to contribute their insight concerning ethics to help create a global ethic. In Buddhist and non-Buddhist ethics, we can find many deep truths. What kind of concrete contribution can Buddhism make toward this effort? We hope the Five Mindfulness Trainings can be a contribution to a global ethic and help provide a way forward for the human species in these dangerous and difficult times.

If we practice the Five Mindfulness Trainings,

we are on a path that will bring us to happiness and the transformation of our own suffering and the suffering of our loved ones. If our practice can be this powerful individually, imagine how powerful it could be if we practiced collectively.

Our lives are more interconnected globally than they have ever been. Our food, our economy, the physical tools we use, our politics cross national and international boundaries. But economics, politics, and education are not the only things being globalized. Our ethics and morality can also be global. We need an ethic that speaks to the whole of humanity. Every culture has unique contributions that they can bring to the creation of a global ethic. And every nation, every people, can contribute aspects of their culture and religion that can make a global ethic something beautiful and appropriate for their country.

DAILY PRACTICE

In order to practice the Five Mindfulness Trainings we need the support of others. If a group meets regularly, then they can support each other. After reciting each training, someone can share how they have practiced that training since the last gathering. It's important not just to talk, but to make sure there is time to breathe in and out mindfully so we can look back at how we have practiced.

In Buddhism there's a practice called the Three Trainings. The Three Trainings are defined as ethics (*shila*), concentration (*samadhi*), and insight (*prajña*). Sometimes they're defined as mindfulness (*smrti*), concentration, and insight. Ethical behavior and mindfulness are very closely connected; they're slightly different approaches to the same thing. When we practice the mindfulness trainings, we refrain from performing actions that we're aware would cause suffering. In order to have this awareness, we need mindfulness in our daily actions. The insights embodied in the mindfulness trainings come from our practice of walking, sitting, breathing, and eating. The Five Mindfulness Trainings come from our own experience of being aware, peaceful, and clear-minded. We're aware that killing brings suffering, so we're determined not to kill, but rather to nourish life. Our own awareness helps us know what to do and what not to do and we can see things in a deeper, more compassionate way.

When we breathe mindfully and walk mindfully we are truly present and we are aware of what is happening in us and around us. We recognize strong emotions and negative states of mind as they arise and we know what we should do and what we should not do. In a difficult or dangerous situation, if we panic we could make many mistakes and things will become much worse. When we are able to come back to our breathing (mindfulness) and stop the confused activities of our mind (concentration), we shall know intuitively what to do and what not to do (insight). The practice of the mindfulness trainings helps us develop concentration and insight. To live our life in mindfulness and with concentration is to continue to produce insight for our own liberation, healing, and nourishment, and for the liberation, healing, and nourishment of the world.

THE ETHICAL AND SPIRITUAL ARE CONNECTED

Recently, I was interviewed by a Christian theologian who asked, "How can we bring about a global spirituality?" But spirituality can't be separated from ethics. There needs to be a relationship between the spiritual and the ethical. If we practice the Five Mindfulness Trainings, we have a practice that is both spiritual and ethical that can guide us collectively toward a more sustainable way of life.

There's a deep link between the ethical and the spiritual. If you can't see the spiritual in the ethical, your ethic may be empty. You may do things without knowing why and there may be no joy in your actions. For example, inspired by the Fifth Mindfulness Training, you may decide not to drink alcohol or use drugs. But if you resent the training, and you suffer because you still want to drink alcohol or use drugs, the ethic that you follow is empty, because you don't really see the value of it. The mindfulness trainings are based in insight and love, not on prohibition and withholding. The same is true with any of the trainings. If you're a vegetarian because you think you should be, but you wish that you could eat meat, then you aren't really following the trainings. But if you feel that you're lucky to be able to eat primarily vegetables and legumes and to not be causing suffering to other living beings, then there's joy, insight, compassion, and spirituality in your eating. Eating becomes a very spiritual thing. There's no barrier dividing the ethical and the spiritual.

PRACTICING WITHOUT DOGMA OR RIGIDITY

The Five Mindfulness Trainings are an offering that doesn't contain dogma, religion, or sectarianism. Each of us can use the trainings as practical ethical principles for our life without being part of any particular faith or tradition. You can just be yourself, but try to make your life beautiful by following the wisdom of these trainings. The Five Mindfulness Trainings are, for each of us, the result of our own deep looking and of the collective deep looking.

The purpose of the trainings is not to follow them perfectly and then feel superior about following them. The trainings are a guide; it's not possible to practice them so perfectly that we prevent any suffering at all. For example, it's not possible to avoid killing. The cultivation of vegetables, the purification of the water we drink, and other necessary human activities cause the death of small living beings. The vegetables, too, are living things. Compared with the suffering of animals, it seems that the suffering of plants is less; but it's not the case that there's no suffering. We can't abolish suffering altogether, but we try to reduce it. We can try to reduce the suffering a little bit every time, every day. The Five Mindfulness Trainings are there to study, to learn about, to recite, and to practice so we can deepen our experiences and understanding, and so we can share that with other people. If we do this as a big community, insight will grow and that will profit many people. If during your practice of the Five Mindfulness Trainings you feel that your compassion and loving kindness have become bigger, that your understanding has grown, that you can share your insight and make things better, then you are on the right path.

Our ethic needs to be an ethic without dogmas, without views. No one imposes the trainings on us, no one is asking us to practice. We ourselves can see based on our own insight and experience that it is our path of joy, compassion, and love. The Five Mindfulness Trainings include the practice of not being caught in a dualistic way of seeing things. Dualism is the view that good and evil, holy and profane, happiness and suffering oppose each other and that it is only by destroying evil that we have good and by destroying the profane that we have the sacred. According to the insight of interbeing, good and evil inter-are. Good is a skillful way of dealing with evil that leads to transformation. It is not something we fight against. Good and evil are organic and are present together. This insight is the only way we can remove all discrimination and fear. It is the foundation of the practice of the trainings. Then the trainings very naturally become the way we live and the source of our happiness.

COLLECTIVE KARMA

In Buddhism there is the notion of karma, which means action. This includes the act of thinking, the act of speaking, and the act of performing physical action. Every thought that you produce is your continuation. Every word that you speak is your continuation. Everything you do with your body is your continuation. Even our thoughts are a kind of energy that we produce. We produce energy in the way that a cloud produces rain. Rain is an action performed by the cloud; the cloud is transformed into the rain. We are very much like the cloud. Just as the cloud produces rain, we produce thought, speech, and actions that will continue us forever. When this body disintegrates, you are continued always by your karma.

You don't need to wait for the disintegration of your body to be reborn in new forms of life. A cloud doesn't need to disappear completely in order to become rain. It's wonderful to be a floating cloud but it's also very wonderful to be the falling rain. When I look around outside me, I see myself in many directions. I have been reincarnated already in many forms. If you think that I'm only here in this body, that's a wrong view; you have not really seen me. We are more than what we can see. We produce many thoughts, words, and actions, and they continue us a little bit everywhere.

With the practice of the Five Mindfulness

Trainings, we can assure that our continuation is contributing to a more sustainable and peaceful world. *The Mindfulness Survival Kit* is not just for our own survival, it is for the survival of future generations and the planet, today and after our bodies are gone.

We can begin practicing at any time. Yesterday, we may have produced an unkind thought. Today, we can produce another thought that can modify and transform the thought produced yesterday. As soon as today's thought of understanding and compassion is produced, it can counteract the thought of yesterday. With mindfulness we have freedom to change ourselves and to help change the world. Practicing the Five Mindfulness Trainings is not just an individual path, but part of a larger global ethic that can change the direction we are currently heading as a people and as a planet. The trainings are there for all of us, wherever we live, whatever our cultural and spiritual traditions might be. If we can each practice these trainings, individually and together, we will find ourselves hand-in-hand, walking the path together toward a sustainable and more joyful future.

Part 2

A Comparison of Ethical Traditions

Different Ethical Traditions and the Practice of Mindful Observation

In our asking what contribution Buddhism can make to a global ethic, it is useful to look at other non-Buddhist ethical values. When we look like this we shall see what these traditions of ethics have in common with Buddhism and what is different. More important, we have a chance to see the different challenges that human beings have had to face in practicing ethical behavior and what pitfalls have presented themselves to those who want to establish ethical systems. As we look at different ethical systems we also look into meta-ethics, the ground on which ethics is based.

Traditional Judeo-Christianity maintains that God has created the universe and has established universal laws. In this view, when we look into things, we can see the purpose of God in everything. Judeo-Christianity maintains that an omnipotent and loving God created the universe for the human species to live in and then created the human species. The universe has its purpose and its meaning; it is there for God to realize his purpose. Judeo-Christian ethics is based on this worldview. God is the institutor of human ethics. God says what is right and what is wrong, what we should do and what we are forbidden to do. The Ten Commandments come from God.

In Buddhism, the Five Precepts, which the Five Mindfulness Trainings are based on, don't come from a decision of the Buddha but from observations made by the Buddha and by the community around him. The insights that come from that observation are the result of the practice of mindfulness. The awareness of the suffering brought about by killing is the result of mindfulness. We are aware of the fact that wrong views, dualistic views, discrimination, misperception, anxiety, anger, and fear lead people to misunderstand and even kill each other, so we vow to practice the First Mindfulness Training to help us let go of wrong views. If we follow Right View and practice looking with the eyes of nonduality, the eyes of interbeing, we shall be able to protect the lives of humans and other species.

THE FOUR WAYS OF INVESTIGATION

In Buddhism ethics is not a discipline apart from psychology and the natural sciences. In the Manifestation Only teachings of Mahayana Buddhism there is a practice of looking deeply called the Four Ways of Investigation. It applies to the investigation into ethics and into other aspects of life. These are four ways of looking deeply that can help us have Right View.

The **First Investigation** is called Investigation of the Name. Name means designation. Buddha is a designation and so are good and evil. We have to investigate the name and this belongs to the field of semantics. What do we mean by a name, such as Buddha, goodness, or evil? Often we see that the name is a mere designation, or a false designation; it's not the truth of the matter.

There is a practice we can do to help us realize what we mean by the word "Buddha." We begin by saying to ourselves:

Let the Buddha breathe.
Let the Buddha sit.
I don't need to breathe.
I don't need to sit.

In this case the thing that I consider to be my-self goes into the background and the thing that I consider to be the Buddha comes into the fore-ground. When we begin the exercise we look on the Buddha and ourselves as two separate realities. But Buddha is just a name and "I" is just a name. They are both false designations. This is something quite deep. Then we say to ourselves:

The Buddha is breathing.
The Buddha is sitting.
I enjoy the breathing.
I enjoy the sitting.

I feel how the Buddha's breathing is gentle and even. The Buddha's sitting is upright and stable. The third part of the exercise is:

Buddha is the breathing.
Buddha is the sitting.
I am the breathing.
I am the sitting.

The peaceful and gentle breathing is the Buddha. You can't find Buddha outside of the peaceful and gentle breathing. We begin to see what Buddha is made up of: solid sitting and gentle breathing, and so we're no longer caught in the word "Buddha." If you look at a robe, you see there is material, yarn, a shuttle, a weaver, a seamstress; but apart from these things there's no robe. So "robe" is a false designation.

Generally we're caught in false designations. This investigation corresponds in part to the philosophy of Logical Positivism. The philosopher August Comte asked questions such as, "You speak of good. What do you mean by good? You speak of evil. What do you mean by evil? Don't play games with words. Don't let yourself be caught in words. You have to ask: What do you mean by that?" These questions and admonitions are an important aspect of the use and study of semantics.

In Buddhism, the investigation into how we use words is very important. In Buddhism we say that all designations are false designations and we should not be caught in them. According to the practice of investigating the name, we have to let go of the name in order to come to the nature. We let go of the word "robe" in order to discover the nature of a robe.

In Judeo-Christian belief, God the Creator is the ontological ground of the universe. If God is the ontological ground, he is not just the creator but he must also be in the creation, in the creatures themselves. In this light, the name God includes the creator and the creation and we can no longer hold that the creator and the creation are two separate realities.

The Buddhist Prajñaparamita Sutras say that the ground of everything is emptiness. We have to understand the meaning of the word "emptiness." This emptiness is not nothingness; it is interbeing which is the absence of both being and non-being. In Buddhism we could say that the ontological ground is emptiness. Sometimes we call this ground nirvana or suchness. In Buddhism we look for Buddha in ordinary beings. Where do we look for God? We look for God in ourselves and we see that this insight exists in Christianity when we say "God is in our heart."

God and we are not two separate realities. We are in God and God is in us. The creator is in the creature and the creature is in the creator. Many Christian teachers, philosophers, and practitioners have experienced this truth of nonduality. In the Gospel, we learn that the Kingdom of God is a seed in our own heart.

In Buddhism, we talk of the emptiness of transmission. There is no transmitter who is separate from the thing transmitted and the person to whom the transmission is made. The body our parents transmit to us is not something separate from them; they are the body they transmit. We don't receive our parents' body as something separate from ourselves; we are our parents' body. So there is no separately existing body, no separately existing transmitter, and no separately existing inheritor. We can also speak of the emptiness of creation. If there were no creatures, there could not be a creator. We can't recognize God the creator outside of the creation. God is his creation.

In order to transcend the dualism between semantics and ontological ground, there is epistemology, the study of knowledge and belief. In the Zen school we say: "There is a transmission that does not depend on teaching, words, and language. It goes straight to the heart. It is the ability to see the true nature and become Buddha." The heart of Zen is not to be caught in words and language, even in words like "Buddha" and "Dharma." So when we do use words and terms we have to be very careful, whether we're the teacher or the disciple, otherwise both listener and speaker will be caught. Zen is a tradition in which we want to come as close as possible to the truth. The question is, can we use our intellect to do this, or do we just use intuition and direct insight? This is a matter of epistemology.

In Buddhism, there is a kind of wisdom called nondiscriminative understanding. This is the insight that subject and object are not two separate realities but that they lie in each other. The foundation of ethics and of the mindfulness trainings is very deep. If we don't learn to be aware of the limitations of designations and names, we won't be able to understand the trainings deeply and we shall be caught in the words and terms used in the mindfulness trainings.

The **Second Investigation** is the investigation into the meaning or the thing. This means the object of investigation itself, and not the name. When the *bodhisattva* looks, she looks into the thing itself and doesn't need to consider the name. We tend to think of father on the one hand and son or daughter on the other hand as two separate realities. But if we look into our father's five *skandhas* (the five elements of his being: body, feelings, perceptions, mental formations, and consciousness) and into our own five skandhas, we shall see that we are the continuation of our father; we are very much the same as our father.

The **Third Investigation** is the investigation into self-nature (*svabhava*). When we look into the wave we see that its nature is water. When we look into trees, houses, rocks, people, animals, we want to know what is the true nature of all these things. For a long time people have said that things are built out of atoms. They have also said that the ground of things is God, is the Way, is the four great elements of earth, water, fire and air. There are other ideas about the ground of things. Scientists have sought the foundation of things in atoms, the original molecules, and scientists seem to be knocking on the door of ontology—the branch of metaphysics and philosophy that's concerned with the nature of being. In Buddhism it's the same. We see things and we want to find out the true nature of those things. The Heart Sutra is about the ontological ground. The true nature of everything is the nature of no separate self, interbeing.

The **Fourth Investigation** is the investigation into the false establishment of separate realities. The wave is made of water but water is also made of things that are not water. That is true of everything. Everything is made of nonself elements, those things that are not itself. Quantum mechanics has also arrived at the same insight. In the beginning, scientists were looking for atoms and molecules, thinking that they were the foundation of everything. But in fact molecules, atoms, and subatomic particles can only exist in dependence on one another. It's like left and right. What is the right? Is it something real? It seems to be real and so does the left. There is a left-hand side and a right-hand side, but the truth is that the left-hand side cannot be if the right-hand side is not there.

How can we apply this to ethics? When we talk about good and evil, right and wrong, first of all we say that good is a designation that points to certain ways of behavior. Then if we examine the thing itself, the good, we find that it is made of what is not good and at that point we can no longer be dogmatic about what we call good and evil. Buddhist ethics are not dogmatic. In theistic religions people have had the tendency to identify God with the good and Satan with the evil, and the two sides oppose each other. Sometimes in popular Buddhism too there is the tendency to see good as opposing evil, but the original teachings of the Buddha do not see things in this way.

Ethics needs a foundation, and that is provided by the study of meta-ethics. The kinds of questions posed by meta-ethics are: "What is good? What is evil? What is right? What is wrong?" Meta-ethics is concerned with this ground of ethics.

In Buddhist meta-ethics, the ground of reality transcends good and evil, right and wrong. If God is to be identified only with the good, we cannot say that God is the ground of being.

When we talk about good we're talking about behaviors and actions that lead to what we call good. Good is just a designation. It doesn't have an absolute value. The same is true of evil. We all know that without the mud we can't grow lotuses. Therefore to wish to only have lotuses and eliminate the mud isn't very intelligent. Once we remove all the mud no more lotuses will be possible. The view of good and evil in Buddhism is that they are relative concepts. This is the meta-ethics of Buddhism. The nature of reality goes beyond all ideas of right and wrong. Ideas of right and wrong only have relative value. There are two domains:

the domain of nature and the domain of human activity. In the domain of human activity we have established what is right, what is wrong, what is good, and what is bad. These ideas have a practical application and they are purely relative. We can't make these relative values into something absolute and fixed. As far as the ultimate dimension or nirvana is concerned there is no more right, wrong, good and bad. Good and evil are relative ideas like above and below. When we say above and below we have to ask above and below what? If we're in France we say that our feet are below and our head is above. Someone looking from Vietnam would say that our head is below our feet. What we call above would be called below by people on the other side of the world. We can't apply the idea of above and below to the universe, although we can apply it to where we are standing.

It's incorrect to say that the *Dharmakaya*—the teaching of the Buddha—is pure; but it's also incorrect to say that it's impure. Someone asked the eminent Vietnamese Zen master Tue Trung: "What is the purified Dharmakaya?" He replied: "Buffalo dung and cow urine." That was to help people to not be caught in ideas of purity and defilement. Theologians need to learn more about this, so they can let go of old ideas and so their ideas can include the findings of modern science.

Meta-ethics is a very important field of study in our own time, because it can function as the foundation for all ethical theories. Meta-ethics studies and questions the meaning and nature of ethical statements, terms, and evaluations, as well as the assumptions, judgments, and attitudes we make about them. Therefore semantics is an important part of meta-ethics. For example if we're discussing whether God exists or not, we can't get anywhere if we haven't agreed on what is meant by God. We have the word God but everyone understands the word in a different way. We talk about right and wrong, but what is the meaning of the words "right" and "wrong"? And how do we determine what is right or wrong, good or bad? It's like when we say that we practice in order to realize nirvana. Someone may ask us, "What do you mean by nirvana?" Then you have to look to see if you've been entertaining an idea of nirvana that may have nothing to do with reality.

The Dream

One night I dreamed that I was running away from invaders. There will be times when a Vietnamese, Iraqi, or Palestinian person who has lived through war, will dream of running away from an invading army. Even if the war has ended, the terrifying spectacle of people running as bombs fall will sometimes come up in dreams. We are running and all around us there is confusion. In our dream we are not aware that our body is still lying on our bed. We are convinced that we are running away from the bombs. In the dream we have a separate self, a body, and then there is the environment we are in. We believe that all this is real. Only when we wake up do we realize that the dream was not real; the person who was sleeping is real, the bedroom is real, the bedside lamp is real. In that dream, I ran until I came to a place where there were no bombs falling, the road was empty, and I told myself there was no one around, so I could practice walking meditation. I practiced walking meditation in the dream. As I practiced walking meditation, I saw that I was dreaming. That meant that I was about to wake up. The strange thing was that as soon as I began to practice walking meditation I saw that the person walking was an illusion and the surroundings in which I was walking were also an illusion. Then I woke up and I knew that it was all a dream, although in the dream it had seemed to be very real. There was real fear, anxiety, and hurrying away from the bombs. I had already begun to breathe mindfully in the dream. After waking, I continued to breathe mindfully, and I still saw the person lying on the bed and the surroundings as a kind of dream.

It's easy to see that a dream isn't something real. But it's not so easy to see that when we're awake things aren't real in the way we think they are because we're influenced by wrong perceptions and delusion. We think that we're awake but in fact we continue to dream. For example, although we know intellectually that things are impermanent, we live as though our body is permanent.

Philosophers, scientists, and all kinds of religious leaders search for the truth because they do not trust their own perceptions and they have the impression that although they are awake, they're living in a dream. There's someone who has woken up from the second dream and has offered us ways of practice so that we also can wake up from our second dream, and that is Buddha Shakyamuni. Buddha Shakyamuni was a yogi. Buddha means "awakened." When the Buddha awakened he was no longer under the illusion that there was anyone or anything with a separate self-existence, or that the world was something separate from the one perceiving it. We are still living in the second dream but we all have the ability to wake up from it, because we all have the seed of mindfulness. We should have confidence that we are able to wake up from the second dream.

EASTERN ETHICAL TRADITIONS
....

Confucian Ethics

Confucian ethics is concerned with the question of whether man is by nature good or evil. Mencius (third century CE) was a philosopher in the Confucian tradition who believed that humans were by nature good and had an instinctive goodness from the time of birth. Mencius held that goodness is something real and instinctive in everyone.

When asked how he saw the goodness of man, he explained it as four feelings, which are innate in humankind:

1. Feeling of Compassion

We are occupied in some business in our house, and we suddenly see that there is a tiny two-and-a-half-year-old child trying to climb onto the rim of a well. We hurry to the gate of our house but it is locked so we can't run to save the child from falling into the well. We feel extremely uncomfortable, because we didn't save the child, even though it was not our child. That feeling of responsibility for the welfare of the child is instinctive in us. It is unbearable for us to stand to one side while the child drowns. We have no choice but to run to the well and save the child. We don't want to save the child in order to be thanked by the parents, or to become famous, or to receive a reward. Quite automatically that feeling of not being able to bear seeing the child die comes up in us. That is the heart of love. We don't have it as a result of our upbringing or education; it's the instinctive seed of goodness in us all.

2. Feeling of Shame

We naturally feel ashamed of doing what is wrong. That is something instinctive in us from the time we are born. The equivalent to this in Buddhism is the two wholesome mental formations *hri*, shame in our self, and *apatrapya*, shame before others. According to Mencius, as long as we have a sense of shame we can be a good person. The feeling of shame that arises when we do something wrong is quite instinctive. We don't have to train in order to have it. In Buddhism shame in oneself and shame before others are two of the eleven wholesome mental formations that arise from seeds in the store consciousness. These mental formations help us to recognize when we're going on a path of suffering and to be able to change our direction.

shame as an attitude

3. Feeling of Compliance and Deference

All people have the ability to let go of their attachments to particular ideas, in order to be able to live in harmony with society and others. According to Confucius we should know our position and act in accord with that. If we are a father we should act as a father and if we are a son we have to be a son.

4. Feeling of Right and Wrong.

Humans have the capacity to distinguish right from wrong. Animals don't have that capacity, or it's still in the store consciousness and doesn't manifest clearly.

Mencius believed that humans and other animals were not very different from one another. The only difference, according to Mencius, is the instinctive goodness of humans that animals don't have. Because of this goodness, human beings have established ethical behavior.

Other philosophers have very pessimistic views of the human race. They say that on the outside it looks as if people have virtue, but when we look into this virtue, we find that it is just egotism. Everyone is just looking out for him or herself. There was another philosopher in China, named Xunzi (c. 310 – c. 238 BCE), who believed that humans weren't good by nature. He held that humans are born evil and he "proved it" saying, "Looking at a baby, you can see its greed, anger, selfishness, and jealousy." In a baby all the unwholesome characteristics can be observed and, thanks to education and training, the unwholesome diminishes.

According to the Manifestation Only teachings of Buddhist psychology there is a store consciousness that is made of all the seeds (*bija*). Human beings have all the good seeds and all the evil seeds, so the store consciousness is described as having all the seeds (*sarvabijaka*). Store consciousness is not good or evil; the good and evil seeds inter-are. Human beings are not by nature good or evil, since all the seeds are available in store consciousness. When seeds are watered they arise in mind consciousness. Practicing mindfulness, we have the ability to choose which seeds we water and to transform latent tendencies, which cause certain seeds to arise. Without training and the right environment it is very difficult or impossible to do this.

Taoist Ethics

In Taoist thinking, there is the idea of the Way (*dao*) as the ground. In traditional Judeo-Christian religion, the Creator God is referred to as male. In Taoism, the Way is looked on as female, a mother. The Way is the mother of all things in heaven and on Earth.

Laozi lived at about the same time as the Buddha Shakyamuni. In the Dao Te Jing of Laozi there's a verse: "There is something that comes about by mixing. It arose before the heaven and the Earth; it is very peaceful and silent. It penetrates everywhere without growing tired. I do not know its name, but for want of a better name call it dao and I cannot describe it. For want of a better description I call it great. It could be considered as the mother of heaven and Earth."

Another Chinese philosopher and Taoist master, Zhuangzi (c. 369 – c. 286 BCE) went further than Laozi. He said that the heavens and the Earth and we ourselves depend on each other to manifest, and all things in the universe are one with us. Without us, there would be no heaven and Earth and without heaven and Earth there would be no us. This insight is very close to interbeing and the Buddhist way of looking.

Laozi believed that the innate nature of humans is neither good nor evil. If we train someone in the direction of goodness he will be good, and if we train him in the direction of evil he will be evil. It's like a stream of water. If you direct it to the east it will flow to the east and if you direct it to the west it will flow to the west. It is true that if you dig a trench in the easterly direction the water will flow to the east. The teachings of Laozi and Zhuangzi transcend good and evil, in the same way as the Buddhist Prajñaparamita Sutra maintains there is no defiled and no immaculate. Taoism and Buddhism are in accord on this matter.

In the Manifestation Only teachings, good and evil are recognized as seeds and if these seeds don't have the right conditions to manifest, they remain latent in store consciousness and grow weaker. The seeds of anger and violence are always present in store consciousness, but when we live in a very wholesome environment and everyone around us behaves in a well-mannered, courteous, and loving way, those seeds of violence and anger won't have much chance to manifest. On the other hand, if we live in an environment where people dispute, are violent, and trick and scheme against each other, the seed of violence, trickery, and scheming in us will be watered and sooner or later we'll become someone with these unwholesome qualities and we'll suffer a great deal. As far

> as the ultimate dimension is concerned there is no
> good and evil, but as far as the phenomenal world
> and our daily lives are concerned there are always
> good and evil, right and wrong, even though these
> things inter-are.

WESTERN ETHICAL TRADITIONS

Utilitarianism

In the West we see ethical systems that are intricately
linked with the idea of God and those that are secular. The ethics of utilitarianism are secular.

Utilitarianism was founded by the lawyer
Jeremy Bentham (1748–1832) and the economist
John Stuart Mill (1806–1873). Both of them
were English philosophers and sociologists. They
had been influenced by the philosophy of the
Scottish historian and philosopher David Hume
(1711–1776). According to utilitarianism, whether
a behavior is good, evil, right, or wrong depends
on whether it is beneficial for the happiness of the
greatest number. In utilitarian ethics, good and
evil actions are not good and evil in themselves but
because of the result of those actions. If the action

leads to suffering it is evil. If it leads to happiness it is good. If an action is for the happiness and benefit of the greater number then it's a good action.

In Buddhism we speak of good and evil in terms of what can lead to enlightenment, liberation, freedom, and the reduction of suffering. In this sense it's relatively close to utilitarianism. Utilitarianism also holds that we shouldn't punish people, because punishment leads to suffering. This shows the compassionate nature of utilitarianism. According to utilitarianism, prisons shouldn't be places where people have to pay for their crimes and suffer, but centers where there are means to give the prisoners a chance to reform, such as libraries, classes, technical schools. Although people have tried to reform prisons in this way, up to now it hasn't been widely successful.

In former times, in Vietnam, China, and Korea, the Buddhist temples used to ask for prisoners who had been sentenced to ten or twenty years of imprisonment to be released to their custody. The monks would take responsibility for helping the criminals to transform, so they would be allowed to take one or two prisoners back to the temple. They would ask the prisoners to work for the temple, for example to work in the rice fields. The monks would keep an eye on the prisoners, ask them to come to the recitation of the Five Mindfulness Trainings every fortnight, to follow a vegetarian diet at least four times a month, and to attend Dharma talks. The temple would take care of them when they were sick. The monks would listen to them and give them advice. It meant that the temple really wanted to help that person and not just use them as a manual worker. In the case that the prisoner had transformed and was of marriageable age, the temple could also arrange for him to marry into a local farming family.

After the monks had shown that the prisoner had truly transformed, the government or correctional authority would grant him his freedom and he could continue to work for the temple or he could go and settle on his own farm. It was a successful way of reforming prisoners and it follows the line of utilitarianism. The proposal of utilitarianism in the eighteenth century was already being carried out in Asian Buddhist temples one thousand years before. The idea is that we don't want to punish; we want only to help. Out of delusion and anger, a criminal has broken the law. We want him to feel regret for what he has done and begin anew, but we don't need to make him suffer. So instead of locking him in a dark cell, we allow him to work in the fields, breathing the fresh air and learning the practice of transformation.

Utilitarianism is simple enough. First of all we have to say what we want for people: employment, food, clothes, harmony in the family, freedom, human rights, peace, and so on. Once we have listed humanity's needs, we need to find the appropriate actions to realize them. All actions that lead to people having enough to eat, clothes to keep warm, human rights, and protection are good actions. This is consequentialism, which says that an action is determined to be right or wrong based on its consequences.

In Buddhism when we say there is an end of ill-being (happiness, well-being) and a path that leads to the end of ill-being, this is also consequentialism. Buddhism also says that everything that belongs to the Fourth Noble Truth, the Noble Eightfold Path, and that leads to the end of ill-being is good and right. The difference between Buddhism and utilitarianism is that utilitarianism does not explain the interbeing nature of suffering and happiness.

When we list the things that count as happiness for humankind, some people will say that full employment is the most important thing; others will say the protection of the environment or human rights is most important. It would take a great deal of wisdom to list in order of importance the things that are needed for human happiness. For example, if President Obama were to try to list in order of importance what should be done for human happiness, should he choose first to resolve the economic crisis, stop businesses from going bankrupt, stop businesses from laying off workers, end involvement in Afghanistan or Iraq without delay, or reduce the tension between the United States and Iran? When it has been decided what to go ahead with first, he has to find the way to deal with that particular issue. Whatever action leads to resolving the issue can be termed a good action.

One of the principles of utilitarianism is to help everyone see that what matters is the happiness of the greatest number. If something leads to our own happiness and harms others, it's not good. We have to give our attention to what makes others happy. So the element of letting go is found in utilitarianism. We need someone who is able to see what is the greatest happiness of the greatest number and that person is called the ideal observer. Realistically, it will be very difficult to find this ideal observer. As Buddhists we could say that Buddha Shakyamuni is that ideal observer, and as students of the Buddha we must do our best as far as the Buddha's teachings are concerned to find the most important happiness for the greatest number. Christians could say that Jesus Christ is the ideal observer and that they would do their best as disciples of Christ to find what is the most important happiness for the greatest number. However, utilitarianism and consequentialism are not interested in including God and the holy scriptures in their systems of ethics. They only trust in the reasoning of humankind based on human experience.

In the world we see that there are many people who have plenty to eat and more than enough clothes to wear, yet they still suffer deeply, sometimes enough to commit suicide. What these people need most of all is to cultivate love and understanding. In Buddhism we see that the thing people need most of all is inner peace and the capacity to love and understand. The reason why we practice Buddhism is not because we want someone to give us food, clothes, freedom of speech, and social justice, but because we want to be able to produce understanding and love in our own hearts. We know that when we have love and understanding in our hearts, the matter of enough food, warm clothes, and social justice for everyone will be much easier to solve. As far as the Buddha is concerned, the first things on the list are understanding, love, tolerance, and forgiveness.

As Buddhists we say that suffering plays a part in bringing about happiness. It means that all of us need a certain amount of suffering to grow up and be happy. But how should we measure the amount of suffering that we need? Actually, no one wants to suffer. In the Buddhist tradition a bodhisattva is someone who always helps relieve others of their suffering. A bodhisattva knows that suffering can be the result of unskillful action, but never says: "You have to bear it; you are the one who sowed the seed so you have to bear the consequence. Why should I help you?" A bodhisattva always wants to help people who have fallen into a state of suffering. Suppose one day the car of a selfish (as you see him) neighbor breaks down and he asks you to give him a lift to work. If you think in terms of retribution, and want to punish him for his past selfish actions, you would say to yourself: "This difficult gentleman, why should I care whether he gets to work or not? Let him be late for work as he deserves." According to utilitarianism, if we see someone in difficulty and we abandon him, that's not right. So we say: "Okay, hop in the car." We don't punish him; we use our heart of compassion to help him. Often if we don't punish but are kind, it helps the other person to change. We set an example of tolerance, which helps the other to be less selfish. A bodhisattva goes more in the direction of utilitarianism, which holds that life has quite enough suffering already, so why should we add to it by punishing each other? Of all the Western ethical systems, we could say that utilitarianism is most close to Buddhism.

Retributivism

According to this theory, if people don't have to suffer for the harm they've done to others, they'll never understand the harm they've done. If you kill, you have to pay for it with your life. If you beat, you have to be beaten. The practical reasons that are given are that if someone commits a crime and isn't punished, then the family of the victim will continue to suffer, and if the criminal is punished the family will feel avenged and have no more feelings of being the victims of injustice. The second reason for punishing is that if the person is not punished, he will continue to commit crimes harming others; so punishment is seen as a deterrent. The third reason is to deter others from committing the same kind of crime. We all have this tendency within us of wanting to treat good people better than we treat bad people. In the Sutra in Forty-two Chapters there's the sentence: "When offerings are made to a good person the merit is ten times greater than when offerings are made to a bad person. Offerings made to an enlightened Buddha are worth one thousand times the merit of offerings made to an unenlightened person."

Looking into this reasoning, we see that it is not a matter of equanimity but a matter of investment. We are practicing generosity when we make offerings. The practice of generosity means that when people are hungry we give them something to eat, and when they suffer we help them. We do not calculate what the benefit of helping one person will be as opposed to the benefit of helping another. According to this sutra, generosity can be a kind of investment, not an investment for our own profit but an investment for the world. If we save the life of a good person, that person will continue to help others. If we save the life of a bad person, although we are helping that person not to suffer, it may mean that that person continues to make others suffer. Of course a bad person can always transform, so we also save his life, but here the word "merit" means the happiness that results from helping a good or enlightened person is generally much greater than that which results from helping someone bad or unenlightened. Ethics is not always an easy subject to understand. We have to observe the mind in the way we behave and know what our motivation is. If our behavior is motivated by the desire to punish we could say it is not Right Action based on Right Thinking. If our motivation is to help a community or a number of individuals to be a refuge and help for many others, then we could say it is based on Right Thinking.

Imagine you have two neighbors. One of them is very kindhearted, always ready to lend a helping hand. The other is very difficult, narrow and selfish. When the two of them come and ask you to lend them something, you feel very ready to give it to the kindhearted neighbor because you feel she deserves it. As for the other neighbor, you hem and haw, or you say outright that you can't lend it, because you think that this is a chance to teach him a lesson. To a greater or lesser degree, we all have the tendency to follow the ethics of retributivism.

Ethical Egoism

This is not as bad a system of ethics as it sounds. It also has its insight. People who follow this line of thinking say that we have to take care of ourselves first and that is the basis. They say that we only live once, so we need to live happily, and what is the point of caring about society. The idea is that we take care of our own happiness and security before anything else. If we look deeply we shall understand this egoism in the sense of no-self. For example, if we cheat and defraud people because we want to take their money, no one will trust us and no one will want to trade with us anymore. If everyone boycotts us, we shall fail in our desire to make money. An egoist has to be honest; if he trades fairly, he will benefit. When we make ourselves truly happy, that benefits others as well.

If we breathe in, we just take care of breathing for ourselves, we don't need to breathe for anyone else. We breathe out and we release the tension in our body. We may think we're doing this uniquely for ourselves. If we're successful and we manage to relax, we're no longer bad-tempered or displeased, but happy and peaceful, and others will benefit from our freshness. So looking after our own needs is not necessarily something bad or selfish. If we don't each take care of our own body and mind and we allow the unwholesome energy to affect those around us, that can hardly be called ethical conduct. It may look selfish when we do walking meditation for ourselves, but the peace and joy we feel as a result are also for others and for our world.

Sometimes Mahayana Buddhists say that those who practice according to the Theravada tradition are only interested in their own enlightenment and liberation and not in the enlightenment of all beings. However, if a practitioner of the Theravada tradition practices Theravada Buddhism correctly, that is already the Mahayana because he's practicing for everyone.

An egoist wants to be happy and therefore needs to know what real happiness is. Looking deeply, we know that the greatest happiness comes when we have loving kindness in our hearts and we can bestow that loving kindness on others. When we are angry and feel no love, we can't be happy, even if we have wealth, security, and a high position in society.

A monk, nun, or lay practitioner can be called an egoist, because he or she devotes a great deal of time to developing her mind so that every day she becomes more at ease, more tolerant, and more loving. When he can smile in difficult moments, the whole world benefits. So egoism is not necessarily a bad thing.

Ethics of Altruism

This is the opposite of the ethics of egoism. It maintains that we should not look out for ourselves, but only care for others. Our self is not important.

There are people who for the whole of their lifetime only care for others. When they protect or take care of themselves they don't feel happy, but when caring for others their heart overflows with joy. At that point the boundary between self and other is no longer there. Although it looks as if the ethics of egoism and the ethics of altruism contradict each other, in fact they're very close to each other. In the light of the Buddhist teachings we see that the terms egoism and altruism are based on the idea of a separate self. In fact, you and I inter-are. Looking into myself I see you and looking into you I see myself. That is the teaching of no-self. In the light of no-self, the ethics of altruism and the ethics of egoism are one and the same. Just as with utilitarianism, these two see that any action that leads to people's happiness, our own and that of others, is right or good.

Consequentialism

Utilitarianism, the ethics of altruism, and egoism are consequentialist ethics. People say that the ethics of consequentialism are difficult to follow because they don't tell us what behavior is in itself good or evil. There's no real definition of good and evil. We can only say whether the action is good or evil when we know its result.

The term consequentialism was invented by the English philosopher Elizabeth Anscombe (1919–2001) for a kind of ethics with which she did not agree. According to consequentialism, we can do anything if it has a good result. If the result is good then the action is good and the end justifies the means. Since peace is a good result, then dropping two atomic bombs and killing 210,000 people immediately and causing many more to die as a result of radioactive fallout is right. When we hear this kind of reasoning, we don't feel comfortable and we can't sleep peacefully. After the Second World War and the dropping of the atomic bombs,

Elizabeth Anscombe and her fellow students knelt down in prayer to protest against President Truman being awarded an honorary doctorate by Oxford University.

Let's say there's someone who's addicted to gambling. He's lost all his money, so he wants to borrow more so he can continue gambling. He knows that if he tells the truth about why he needs the money no one will lend it to him so he lies and says: *Please do me a favor and lend me some money. My wife is ill; my children are hungry. I assure you I'll pay you back as soon as I can.* If we think consequentialism gives us permission to lie in this way, it's quite dangerous.

Deontology

Deontology is the ethics of duty or obligation; it's also called rule-based ethics. This is the principle of ethics held by Immanuel Kant, that there are principles of right and wrong that don't depend on the consequences. For example not killing people is good in itself; telling the truth is good in itself. We don't need to know anything about the result of the action of not killing or of not telling the truth to be able to judge that they are good actions. Even if by killing someone we reduce suffering, it's still not good. There are certain things that we can never do, whatever the consequence may be.

There was a scientist by the name of E. W. Caldwell who studied X-rays for thirty years. At the time people didn't know enough about the dangers of X-rays, so he didn't protect himself from radiation and became seriously ill as a result. At one point the doctors said that he could live for another three months. But he was in a great deal of pain, so he asked his three brothers to help him die as quickly as possible. His two elder brothers refused to kill him, even though that was what he wanted most of all. The younger brother felt tremendous pity for his brother who was suffering. He came to the hospital with a gun and shot him five or six times and he died. That killing came from compassion. According to the law he had to be sentenced. But the judge understood and gave him a light prison sentence.

In Italy, there was the case of a thirty-eight-year-old woman who for eighteen years had lain in bed in great pain because of a disease. She wanted to die. Her father also wanted her to die so that she wouldn't have to suffer so much pain, but the law of the land didn't allow it. After many campaigns the high court secretly gave permission. Father and daughter were very glad and when he came home to her, he disconnected the tubes that were keeping her alive and a few days later she could die.

However, the governments of some countries are working with the Vatican to make laws to forbid this kind of killing. This leads to tension between the courts, the legislature, and the Church. This is one of the most important ethical issues of our time. Deontologists rigidly refuse to look at the consequences. They see suffering, they know there is suffering, but there's nothing we are allowed to do about it, even for the sake of humane action.

Buddhism isn't rigid in its approach to ethics. In Buddhism we have the criteria of opening or barring the way. President Truman allowed the atomic bomb to be dropped on Hiroshima. In a few minutes 140,000 people died, and hundreds of thousands of people were affected by radioactive fallout and later died as a result. A few days later, the second atomic bomb was dropped on Nagasaki and 70,000 more people died. Of course, to drop the bomb may or may not end the war. We cannot know; we can't be certain about it. But what is certain is that many people will die. But the question is more complicated. Maybe those who have fabricated the bomb are eager to see the effect of the bomb. Maybe politicians hope that after the bomb is dropped, people will acknowledge the United States as the one superpower, the nation that no other nation can defeat. So there may be a desire and an attempt to show that the United States is the most powerful nation. There may be that kind of thinking and desire in the minds of the political advisors. A president has many military and political advisors, but he needs a good community that can represent the kind of wisdom and courage that can help him not to give up his principled stand. When many people keep saying the same thing, keep talking with the same persuasive kind of language, it's very powerful, and you risk following their advice against your better judgment; especially when, after having debated for many days, you are very tired. For such a big problem we can't pretend to have an easy answer. We need the collective wisdom. We especially need the collective compassion. An act that's wise needs to have the element of compassion in it. Sometimes you think only of the goal, and you think that any means of achieving that end is justified and good. But in the Buddhist tradition we know that means and ends are the same thing. "There's no way to peace; peace is the way." If the means aren't peaceful, then you're not doing peace. If the way you think, speak, and act isn't peaceful, the outcome won't be real peace. People are still discussing the morality of the dropping of nuclear bombs on Japan at the end of World War II. According to some politicians it was the right thing to do, because they believe this was what brought the Second World War to an end.

Virtue Ethics

This theory says that certain qualities such as compassion, joy, and tolerance are moral. You don't need to know the result of the action. Compassion is always something good. There are these good qualities, and as a human being we have to nourish them in ourselves, whatever the result may be. There is a great deal of truth in this. It looks as if there is a contradiction between consequential-ism and virtue ethics, but that's not necessarily so. For instance we nourish compassion in ourselves, although we don't yet know what the consequence of this will be (this is the practice of virtue ethics). As soon as we feel compassion, we no longer suffer very much (this is the consequence). On the other hand, if our heart is filled with anger and hatred we suffer a great deal. So we can see the result of compassion as soon as it arises and the result of anger as soon as it arises in ourselves, and we don't have to wait to see the result on the other person.

Confucian ethics is virtue ethics. One of the principle virtues to be developed by a Confucian is humaneness. In the Analects, Confucius answers the questions of his disciples about humaneness and he defines humaneness as follows: "When you have stood on your own two feet, you help others to stand on their own two feet."

Also according to Confucius, humaneness implies five elements:

1. Loving kindness, compassion, and tolerance. Loving kindness means making others happy. Compassion is relieving others of their suffering. Tolerance is openness and inclusiveness.
2. Respect. We should respect ourselves, have self-esteem and then we have to respect others. Without respect there is no humaneness.
3. Honesty. We have to speak the truth.
4. Diligence.
5. Granting others favors, offering our own virtue to others.

Apart from this there is the famous injunction of Confucius: *Do not do to others what you do not want others to do to you.* For instance we don't like to suffer, therefore we don't cause others to suffer. We don't like to feel regret so we don't make others feel regret. We don't want to starve so we don't cause others to starve.

According to Buddhism we should understand what we mean by *not wanting.* For instance, when a child is sick her mother has to give her medicine. The child doesn't want to take the medicine but her mother forces her to do so because she knows that it's the best thing for the child. There are people who do not want to practice the mindfulness trainings. They know that it's not good to drink alcohol, take drugs, or commit adultery. Every formula to describe ethical behavior has its drawbacks and its value is only relative.

Divine Command

Now we come to the kind of ethical behavior that is linked to a belief in God. Elizabeth Anscombe followed the divine command theory. This means the good and the wholesome is ordered by God and all we need to do is follow it. This sounds very easy. Consequentialism involves reasoning, but divine command is just something we follow. We don't have to weary ourselves by making our own decisions.

There was a family who lived in an island in the Mediterranean, and they went to England for the lady to give birth to twins at a hospital in Manchester. The bigger twin was called Jody; the smaller one Mary. They were conjoined twins and the two girls had only one set of lungs, one heart. They were linked together at the lower abdomen and by the spinal column. People knew that if they weren't stillborn, they would die a few weeks after being born. When the twins were born, the doctors knew they could both survive for only three or four weeks. Jody, the larger twin, had the set of lungs in her body as well as the heart which sent the blood to nourish her twin sister. The staff in the hospital advised the couple to allow a surgery to take place that would separate the two, so they could save at least one child, Jody. In that case, Mary would die. Without the surgery, both of them would die after four weeks.

The couple were devout Catholics and they didn't want to kill. So they told the doctor that everything should be left in the hands of God. Nature should be left to take its course and the parents would not decide. The doctors didn't agree. They said that it was possible to save the life of at least one twin and they took the matter to court. The court allowed them to do the surgery. They saved Jody, and of course Mary died. According to the ethics of divine command, if God wants both of them to die, then you have to allow both of them to die. If you kill one, the other will survive. If you kill neither, both will die. If you're rigid in your belief that intentional killing is wrong, then you wouldn't allow the surgery to take place, and both the children would die. If you follow the line of thinking that at least you can save one of the two and you can accept the death of Mary, then you will feel that that is the best thing to do.

In Buddhism there isn't anything equivalent to divine command. We have the First Noble Truth of suffering, the Second Noble Truth of the origin of suffering, the Third Noble Truth of the extinction of suffering, and the Fourth Noble Truth of the path that leads to the extinction of suffering. This is a kind of consequentialism. If we don't want suffering, we shouldn't create the conditions that allow suffering to arise. If we want the extinction of suffering, we have to follow the path that leads to the extinction of suffering. Anything that leads to the extinction of suffering is good, and everything that we do to avoid bringing about suffering is correct. It seems to be clear that the teaching of the Four Noble Truths is consequentialism, but if we go deeper we see that the Four Noble

Truths inter-are, and that suffering and happiness inter-are. Suffering has its role to play in bringing about happiness. If we've lost the electricity and water for a few days, we feel very happy when they come back on again. In Buddhism, suffering plays a special role in making liberation possible. The way Buddhism looks at suffering is rather different from the way other spiritual traditions look at suffering. We don't bear a grudge against suffering, but we look at suffering with the eyes of interbeing. In Christianity people also practice not to have a grudge against suffering. They practice to see suffering as God's will that can help them to grow. Sometimes suffering is very necessary. So we can talk about the "goodness of suffering." We have to discover the happiness in the suffering and nirvana in the cycle of birth and death. We have to find Buddha in ordinary beings. If there are no ordinary beings there will be no Buddha.

Natural Law

In Christianity the theory of divine command is important, but it's not as important as natural law. Aristotle, the Greek philosopher, disciple of

Plato, left us the natural law. Aristotle lived in the fourth century BCE. He was asking about the nature and the function of things in the universe. He said that everything that is has a purpose. We need to ask: "What is this? Of what is it made? What is its function?" For instance we hold up a knife and ask: "What is this?" The answer is: "A knife." Then we ask: "Of what is it made?" The answer is: "It is made of iron." "Where does it come from?" "It was made by the ironsmith." "What is its function?" "Its function is to cut." Aristotle saw that everything in the universe has a reason for being there, a purpose, and it's not here by chance. Moreover, according to natural law we should use things according to their purpose. For example, teeth are made to chew and we should not use them for any other purpose. The purpose of sex is procreation and we shouldn't have sex with any other purpose. For this reason, Catholicism can't accept sex between people of the same gender.

If we ask what eyes are for, the answer is to see. In fact, eyes have other purposes than to see. The look of our eyes can express love or disagreement. Some philosophers oppose this rigid application of natural law by the Catholic Church. We have to become a practical observer, to look deeply, and ask before we decide what kind of action is right and what kind is wrong. When we look with the eyes of interbeing and nonduality we become more flexible.

According to the Church, divine command posits that we cannot take human life, so to abort a fetus or to use contraception is strictly forbidden. The Church is also strictly opposed to euthanasia, or giving someone a chance to die so they don't have to continue to suffer unbearable pain. Sometimes people lie paralyzed on their bed in terrible pain all day and all night; they long to be able to have an injection that will help them end their life in peace. But the Church won't allow it. On the other hand, the Church doesn't object to the execution of criminals or to someone enlisting in the army. It's interesting that when Aristotle was asked the purpose of disease, he was at a loss. Or we might ask: "What is the benefit or purpose of a typhoon or a forest fire?" Such a question is difficult to answer in the light of natural law. When theists are asked this question they're confused, and they may answer by saying that this is God's punishment for his people who have not lived correctly. Natural law clearly has difficulty explaining certain things.

Descriptive Ethics

There is a field of ethics called descriptive ethics. Its function is simply to describe and compare ethical beliefs. People examine, research, and describe what they've discovered about what is considered good and evil in the different ethical systems that are present in their own and other societies. They don't encourage us to follow this or that system or to act or not act in this or that way.

For instance, descriptive ethics might compare slavery in ancient China and how slaves were treated there with how people bought and sold slaves in the west; and what the changes were in society that caused people to change their way of looking at slavery, so that slavery was ultimately abolished. Or descriptive ethics might study and describe family relationships: how parents relate to children, how a mother-in-law relates to her daughter-in-law, and various marriage customs in different societies. This kind of research is very helpful to those of us who want to contribute to creating global ethics.

Prescriptive Ethics

This system of ethics, also called normative ethics, makes suggestions as to how we should behave to have happiness and not to suffer. It's like a doctor who prescribes medicine to a patient and says that while taking this medicine you should not eat spicy foods. The Ten Commandments of Judeo-Christianity belong to prescriptive ethics as do the Five Mindfulness Trainings. Normative ethics are what give us something like a ruler to measure with so that we know what is right. Prescriptive ethics draw a boundary around what is right and what is wrong. Prescriptive and normative ethics do not belong to meta-ethics.

Individual and Collective Karma

According to the teachings of Buddhism, everything has its collective and individual aspects. The sun is something that everyone on Earth experiences, but some places have more sun than others. A meditation practice center is a collective phenomenon, but the people who live there all have differing degrees of happiness. The collective is in the individual. If another person suffers, some of that suffering is in us. If we had behaved more like a bodhisattva, that person would not be suffering so much now. We have been too busy looking after ourselves, we haven't taken the time to take care of him, and now he doesn't have a way out of his suffering. It would be wrong to put all the blame on him for the difficulties he's going through. In his individual karma there is the karma of all of us who live with him. Thanks to our understanding of the interbeing of individual and collective karma, instead of practicing retributivism we can practice the bodhisattva path of compassion and inclusiveness.

APPLIED ETHICS

The ethics of our time should be applied and not theoretical. A recent former president of France has said that we have to bring the study of ethics back into schools, because the understanding of ethics among young people is minimal; they have no spiritual life and no path to go on. In response, a French intellectual said: "Go ahead and teach ethics if you will, but what exactly will you teach?" I think that there are many things we could share with pupils of primary and secondary schools and with university students about ethics. We could share ways of transforming suffering and the Five Trainings, which, by removing references to Buddhism, we can present as texts for study. Applied ethics can be taught in four stages:

1. We learn how to be relaxed and release tension in ourselves.

2. We learn how to breathe and calm ourselves when we have strong emotions.

3. We learn how to keep communication open with relatives and friends and how to restore communication when it has broken down.

4. We learn ways of looking deeply in order to realize interbeing and no-self and to overcome fear.

The ancestral teachers say that Right View is a deep insight into the Four Noble Truths, but the human mind likes to go in search of the truth about the universe. We like going in search of metaphysics or existentialism. Our tendency is to release our mind out into the universe and ask: "What is the origin of the universe? What are the principles that govern the universe?" Because of this kind of questioning we have to have metaphysics and ontology.

The Buddha was very pragmatic. He said: "You do not need to ask questions about what happens after death, how the universe began, when it will end and so on. Bring your mind back to the real situation in which you're living. You have to recognize the suffering that is, discover its cause, and then find a way out of it." We have to be down-to-earth. The Right View the Buddha talks about is not some abstract knowledge about the universe, but insight into the Four Noble Truths. When we first hear about the Four Noble Truths, we think, that's easy enough. In fact, we haven't yet really understood the Four Truths. About a year ago someone asked me, "Thay, have you understood the Four Truths completely?" I replied: "No. I'm still in the process of understanding them."

A deep understanding of the Four Noble Truths demands that we devote a great deal of time and practice to them. Most of us just have an idea of what the Four Truths are. We haven't understood them. We haven't understood the essence of the Four Truths; we haven't seen that they inter-are. If we haven't understood the truth of suffering, then we haven't understood the truth of happiness; and if we haven't understood happiness, then we haven't understood suffering. When we've truly understood the interbeing nature of the Four Noble Truths we shall understand the interbeing nature of everything. Interbeing means: this is that and that is this; this lies in that and that lies in this; without this you cannot have that.

The relationship between father and son is like this. Father and son inter-are. This means that father and son are empty, empty of a separate self. Everything is empty of a separate self. The flower is only there because the sun, the warmth, the light, the cloud, the Earth, the manure, the gardener, and so on, are there. The flower is empty of a separate self but full of the whole universe. If you see the Four Noble Truths as existing separately from each other, you haven't really seen the Four Noble Truths. In the Heart Sutra we read that "ill-being, the cause of ill-being, the end of ill-being, and the path" are all empty of a separate self. The First

Noble Truth is made of the Second, Third, and Fourth Noble Truths. If you take away the Second, Third, and Fourth Noble Truths there will be no First Noble Truth.

The Mindfulness Trainings Are Like the Ocean

A Buddhist practitioner once wrote me a letter saying in part: "Because of an emergency at home I have to leave the retreat early and I shall not be here to receive the Five Mindfulness Trainings. I came here expressly because I wanted to receive the trainings. Please help!" When we want to receive the trainings we want it with our whole heart. From that deep desire comes our Mindfulness Trainings Body, which is like an aura of protection. People who practice the mindfulness trainings do not need to fear; the energy of mindfulness, concentration and insight is always there to protect them.

At the time when I received the full monastic ordination we had to recite our precepts in Chinese. Now we are very fortunate; we can recite our monastic precepts in our own language. I like very much the preface to the monastic precepts from the Dharmaguptaka school. There's a sentence that reads: "The mindfulness trainings are like the ocean. One lifetime alone is not enough to study and to practice them. They are like precious treasures. We never grow tired in their pursuit. It is because we want to protect our sacred inheritance of the true teachings that we have gathered today to hear the recitation of the mindfulness trainings."

When I was a young monk, I liked very much to read the mindfulness trainings but I hadn't yet realized the true immensity of them. Now I can see that the mindfulness trainings have no limit, no end, and that the more we study them the more extensive they become. In the beginning we might say, "Well, the first mindfulness training is about not killing and the second is about not stealing; so what is it that's so difficult about them that we say the precepts are like the ocean, that they are infinite and have no limits?"

If we study the mindfulness trainings properly and deeply, the more we study the more interesting and deep they become. We feel that we could never study them enough, just as when we go to the jewel mountain we never feel that we could carry away all the jewels that are available. If after studying the

Five Mindfulness Trainings we think we've learned all there is to learn, we haven't really been deeply in touch with the trainings. The trainings contain the practices of mindfulness, concentration, and insight. If our practice of the trainings doesn't include mindfulness, concentration, and insight, then they're not mindfulness trainings in the true sense of the word.

The Nature of Reality: Nondualism

The nature of reality goes beyond all ideas of right and wrong. Ideas of right and wrong only have relative value. His Holiness the Dalai Lama has said: "If I see some Buddhist idea that is not in accord with scientific experiment, I am ready to let go of that idea." That is the spirit of demolishing views.

Mahatma Gandhi said in his autobiography that in order to seek the truth, he had to let go of many of his ideas in order to learn something new. That is the spirit of demolishing views. Although Gandhi was not a Buddhist, in his way of life he always displayed the spirit of stretching himself in order to go forward. That is the spirit of scientific discovery: leaving behind the old in order to discover the new. People from the Christian, Jewish, and other religious traditions can also have that attitude. Gandhi wrote that, even as an elder, he was still growing up as far as wisdom was concerned. He wrote that his learning wouldn't stop while his body was disintegrating. This is the spirit in which we study and practice the Five Mindfulness Trainings.

Insight is Right View, and Right View leads to reconciliation and compassion and never leads to discrimination, division, and hatred. It is the insight of interbeing that leads to compassion, and that insight comes from the practice of looking deeply, without wavering, in meditation. Once we have the insight, the practice of the mindfulness trainings becomes something quite natural. It's as though we have a natural immunity so that we don't need to have an injection to immunize us against a certain disease. When we practice the trainings naturally like that, it doesn't demand any special effort; they have become a natural part of our behavior.

The Buddhist view on ethics and spirituality can be summed up in a few lines:

Both subject and object of perception manifest from consciousness according to the principle of interbeing. Humans are present in all things, and all things are present in humans. On the phenomenal level, there seems to be birth, death, being, and nonbeing, but ontologically these notions cannot be applied to reality. The dynamic consciousness is called karma energy. Everything evolves according to the principle of interdependence, but there is free will and the possibility to transform. There is probability. The one affects the all and the all affects the one. Interbeing also means impermanence, nonself, emptiness, karma, and countless world systems. Right View allows Right Action, leading to the reduction of suffering and the increase of happiness. Happiness and suffering inter-are. The ultimate reality transcends notions of good and evil, right and wrong.

Looking at these lines further, we can understand them more deeply.

Both subject and object of perception manifest from consciousness according to the principle of interbeing.
In the Buddhist tradition, we use the word "dharma"

to mean an object of mind, a phenomenon. We use Dharma with a capital D to mean the teachings, the path of practice, or the true nature of things. For example a pen, your eyes, a pumpkin, are objects of mind (dharmas). Our body has six sense organs: eyes, ears, nose, tongue, body, and mind. The object of the six sense organs is the six sense objects: form, sound, smell, taste, touch, and objects of mind. Form is the object of the eyes, sound of the ears, smell of the nose, taste of the tongue, touch of the body, and dharmas are the objects of the mind. Dharmas are anything that we can perceive (phenomena).

When we have a perception, that perception has two aspects: the subject (perceiver) and the object (perceived). The perceiver and the thing perceived manifest together at the same time. When we say that we see, we mean that we see something. The same is true of hearing, smell, taste, touch, and thought. Subject and object are not separate from each other. They depend on each other in order to manifest. This is something that can be very difficult to understand, but it's absolutely basic in the teachings of Buddhism. Only when we've understood this can we truly understand Buddhism.

For example, when we look at a pumpkin, we have to practice to see the pumpkin as an object of our mind and not as something that's separate from our mind. This is also a teaching of nonduality: the perceiver and the perceived are not independent entities; they're closely connected to each other. This practice is a little difficult, but it's something we can realize. In quantum physics scientists have begun to see that their mind affects and is always there in the particle they are observing.

If we're able to put an end to the dualistic way of looking it's because of meditation. In the Sutra on the Four Establishments of Mindfulness, the practice is to meditate on the body in the body, the feelings in the feelings, the mind in the mind, and the objects of mind in the objects of mind. The object is not something that can ever be separated from the mind that observes or meditates upon it.

Humans are present in all things, and all things are present in humans.

We have gone through 4.5 billion years of evolution and our ancestors have reaped fruits of realization that we can now profit from. We also continue to transform for the sake of our ancestors and descendants, and in order to realize new attainments. If we realize freedom, all our ancestors will be liberated and our descendants will benefit. First of all, we have to liberate ourselves from the idea of a separate self.

Our "self" does not just contain time but also space. Time and space inter-are; they're not two separate realities. If in space there is air, warmth, earth, and water, then in us there is also air, warmth, earth, and water. If in space there are all the species of animals, then in us are all the species of animals. The same is true of all the plant and mineral species. If in former lifetimes we were a bird flying in the sky, then in this very moment we are still a bird. We are a human being, but at the same time we are a bird, a rose, a star. This is not poetic imagery. It's a scientific truth that we're made of the stars.

When stars disintegrate they become clouds of dust in the universe. These clouds of dust come together and make the Earth. The first beings begin to appear, one-celled species, then multi-celled species, then plants, then animals; humans are the youngest species on the earth. To say humans are made of the dust of the stars is true. Humans contain the whole universe. The one contains the all. This insight destroys the prison of a separate self.

The Avatamsaka Sutra uses very beautiful images to describe conditioned genesis, dependent co-arising, and interbeing. In this sutra we read that the one contains the all and the all contains the one. Science has also begun to see this truth. If we have a moment of concentration, mindfulness, and insight, then we're in touch with this truth—not by thinking but by experiencing what is a moment of enlightenment. Not only will it make us happy and peaceful, but we shall see that we have done what all our ancestors have wanted us to do.

Karma Energy

Mindfulness, concentration, and insight are the three kinds of energy that we as practitioners are capable of generating in our daily life. Thanks to the practice of mindfulness, your concentration grows, and you can make a breakthrough into reality and gain an insight that will liberate you from all kinds of afflictions. In the Eightfold Path this insight is called Right View. Right View is the kind of insight that is free from all wrong views, such as birth and death, being and nonbeing.

It is sure that we can take care of our future through the way we think, speak, and act. With the practice of mindfulness, concentration, and insight we can purify our minds and assure a better future.

The first form of action is Right Thinking. When you produce a thought that is full of compassion, that thought heals you and heals the world. Without the base of Right View, you can produce thoughts full of hate and despair. If you produce a thought full of anger, that thought begins to destroy you and destroy the world. Wrong thinking that is full of fear, anger, and hatred can lead a person to commit suicide or to kill other people. Good practitioners can produce thoughts of compassion and understanding every day and heal themselves and heal the world. Thinking is action that can help build or destroy the world.

The second form of action is Right Speech. When you say or write something that is full of understanding and compassion, that is Right Speech; what you say or write heals you and heals the other person and the world. Right Speech is characterized by nondiscrimination and is represented by the Fourth Mindfulness Training. You listen and speak in a way that can restore communication and facilitate reconciliation.

The third form of action is Right Action, what you do with your body. Without discrimination, fear, and anger, the actions you perform with your body can help save and protect. If we don't have Right View our action may be characterized by anger, fear, and discrimination, destroying the world and ourselves. With our bodies and minds we produce many thoughts, words, and physical actions every day. In Buddhism this triple action is called karma. The French philosopher Jean-Paul Sartre said: "Man is the sum of his actions." It means you can define a person in terms not of his body and mind, but in terms of his actions. When the body and mind disintegrate, you continue on in your actions, your karma. That is why it's possible to assure a good future by taking care of our actions.

There is free will and the possibility to transform. There is probability.

Because there is free will and the possibility to transform, there is probability. When certain causes and conditions are present, we can predict a result with a fair amount of certainty. For instance, if someone is put in a very unwholesome environment, we can say that person will develop unwholesome characteristics after a time. And when we put that person in a wholesome environment, it's probable that she will be able to transform, but we cannot predict how long and what form the transformation will take. Things don't happen by chance; they happen when the causes and conditions are sufficient for them to happen. We have the free will to participate in creating the right causes and conditions.

On the phenomenal level, there seems to be birth, death, being, and nonbeing, but ontologically these notions cannot be applied to reality.

To say that when your body disintegrates you cease to exist is a wrong view. You are like a cloud, and a cloud can never die. A cloud can become snow or rain or ice, and the quality of the rain, the ice, the snow depends on the quality of the cloud. If the cloud is acid and full of dust, then the rain will be acid and full of dust also. With the practice of mindfulness, concentration, and insight we can purify our actions and assure a better future. In the course of continuation we don't need a separate self. Does the cloud need a self in order to continue as rain or snow?

I think modern science has found something similar to the idea of no-self. There are trillions of cells in our body, and no cell claims to be the boss. All the cells have ways to communicate with each other, and the reality of no-self can be found in the way our bodies function. When neuroscientists look into our brain they see so many neurons, and they say it's like an orchestra without a conductor. The neurons communicate with each other and a decision is made not by one neuron but by all together. The decision is made based on former experiences. Continuation is possible, and that doesn't need a permanent separate self. It's wonderful to notice that in the twenty-first century Buddhism and science can go together and support each other in the practice. There is good science and bad science, good Buddhism and bad Buddhism, and they can help each other in order to bring about better science and a better Buddhism.

The Five Mindfulness Trainings are not based on dogma or commandments. They're based on the insight that you are able to get by yourself, by looking deeply into the heart of reality. Then you can remove all notions like birth and death, being and nonbeing, and you have the guideposts for living an ethical life filled with much happiness.

The ultimate reality transcends notions of good and evil, right and wrong.

When we realize concentration and insight, we can touch the ultimate reality that goes beyond concepts and notions. Following your breathing, you can realize insight. You can see that breathing is taking place and that there is no breather anywhere outside of the breathing. At this point of concentration there's no thought of right and wrong, When we act out of this state of concentration and insight, it's not possible to do things that will make ourselves and others suffer. Touching the ground of reality that is beyond conceptualization is a way of purifying our thoughts and actions.

Related Titles from Parallax Press

Awakening Joy: 10 Steps to Happiness
James Baraz and Shoshana Alexander

Breathe, You Are Alive!
The Sutra on the Full Awareness of Breathing
Thich Nhat Hanh

Buddha Mind, Buddha Body:
Walking Toward Enlightenment
Thich Nhat Hanh

Happiness: Essential Mindfulness Practices
Thich Nhat Hanh

Mindfulness in the Garden: Zen Tools for Digging in the Dirt
Zachiah Murray

Mindful Movements: Ten Exercises for Well-Being
Thich Nhat Hanh

Not Quite Nirvana: A Skeptic's Journey To Mindfulness
Rachel Neumann

Parallax Press is a nonprofit publisher, founded
and inspired by Zen Master Thich Nhat Hanh.
We publish books on mindfulness in daily life and
are committed to making these teachings acces-
sible to everyone and preserving them for future
generations. We do this work to alleviate suffering
and contribute to a more just and joyful world.

Parallax Press
P.O. Box 7355
Berkeley, CA 94707
Tel: (510) 525-0101

Monastics and laypeople practice the art of mindful living in the tradition of Thich Nhat Hanh at retreat communities worldwide. To reach any of these communities, or for information about individuals and families joining for a practice period, please contact:

Plum Village
13 Martineau, 33580 Dieulivol, France
www.plumvillage.org

Magnolia Grove Monastery
123 Towles Rd., Batesville, MS 38606
www.magnoliagrovemonastery.org

Blue Cliff Monastery
3 Mindfulness Road, Pine Bush, NY 12566
www.bluecliffmonastery.org

Deer Park Monastery
2499 Melru Lane, Escondido, CA 92026
www.deerparkmonastery.org

The Mindfulness Bell, a journal of the art of mindful living in the tradition of Thich Nhat Hanh, is published three times a year by Plum Village. To subscribe or to see the worldwide directory of Sanghas, visit www.mindfulnessbell.org

 planting seeds of Compassion

If this book was helpful to you, please consider joining the Thich Nhat Hanh Continuation Fund today.

Your monthly gift will help more people discover mindfulness, and loving speech, which will reduce suffering in our world.

To join today, make a one-time gift or learn more, go to: www.ThichNhatHanhFoundation.org.

Or copy this form & send it to:
Thich Nhat Hanh Continuation and Legacy Foundation
2499 Melru Lane, Escondido, CA USA 92026

○ **Yes!** I'll support Thich Nhat Hanh's work to increase mindfulness. I'll donate a monthly gift of:
   ○ $10 ○ $30 *($1 a day)* ○ $50 ○ $100 ○ $_____ *Other*

○ Please debit my bank account each month. I've enclosed a blank check marked "VOID".

○ Please charge my credit card each month.

Your Name(s) _____

Name on Card/Account _____

Credit Card No. _____ Exp. Date _____

Address _____

City_____ State/Prov _____ Zip/Postal_____

Country_____ Email _____